EVERYMAN'S LIBRARY
POCKET POETS

ROMAN ODES ELEGIES AND EPIGRAMS

SELECTED AND EDITED BY
PETER WASHINGTON
WITH ILLUSTRATIONS FROM
THE EDITION OF HORACE
PUBLISHED BY JOHANNES PINE,
LONDON 1737

EVERYMAN'S LIBRARY
POCKET POETS

This selection by Peter Washington first published in
Everyman's Library, 1997

© David Campbell Publishers Ltd., 1997

A list of acknowledgments to copyright owners can be found at the back of
this volume.

ISBN 1-85715-734-6

A CIP catalogue record for this book is available from the British Library

Published by David Campbell Publishers Ltd.,
79 Berwick Street, London W1V 3PF

Distributed by Random House (UK) Ltd.,
20 Vauxhall Bridge Road, London SW.1V 2SA

Typography by Peter B. Willberg

Typeset by AccComputing, Castle Cary, Somerset

Printed and bound in Germany by
Graphischer Grossbetrieb Pössneck GmbH

CONTENTS

FOREWORD

Though a fiercely tribal nation, the English have always been surprisingly open to outside influences, especially in their poetry. Perhaps this is less of a paradox than it seems. While a secure sense of linguistic and geographical identity gave them the confidence to take what they wanted from other societies, an awareness of cultural inferiority encouraged the imitation of foreign models.

Whatever the cause, translation has always been vital to the development of English literature. No single body of work has been more important in this process than Roman poetry. In the seventeenth and eighteenth centuries especially, this was translated over and over again, as almost every major poet tried his hand at Virgil and Horace, Ovid, Lucretius and Catullus.

The purpose of my anthology is to offer a selection of these translations while at the same time providing a selective survey of Latin verse. Not all the writers included come from the first rank. Some can be regarded as amateurs in the best sense. Just as Rome bred superb gentlemen poets, Britain produced generations of fine translators, trained by a classical education which encouraged them to pursue translation in later life as a serious amusement.

The popularity of Roman poets has fluctuated over time. The Elizabethans were fascinated by Ovid, the Augustans by Horace; Virgil has remained a constant if understated passion; Propertius has come into his own only in the present century. These changes are reflected in the selection of translators. My choice of poems has largely (though not entirely) excluded satire and epic in favour of lyrical and discursive verse. In one or two cases I have offered different versions of the same poem, either because I could not bear to exclude them or because of the fascinating light they throw on the relationship between literatures. It hardly needs saying that almost every item could have been replaced three or four times over without loss of quality.

PETER WASHINGTON

ROMAN ODES ELEGIES AND EPIGRAMS

LUCRETIUS

From DE RERUM NATURA:
Address to Venus

Great Venus, Queene of Beautie and of grace,
    The joy of Gods and men, that under skie
    Dost fayrest shine, and most adorne thy place;
    That with thy smyling looke doest pacifie
    The raging seas and makst the stormes to flie:
        Thee, Goddess, thee the winds, the clouds doe
            feare;
    And when thou spredst thy mantle forth on hie
      The waters play, and pleasant lands appeare,
And heavens laugh, and all the world shews joyous
        cheare.

Then doth the dædale earth throw forth to thee
    Out of her fruitfull lap aboundant flowres;
And then all living wights, soone as they see
    The spring break forth out of his lusty bowres,
    They all doe learne to play the Paramours;
      First doe the merry birds, thy pretty pages,
    Privily priked with thy lustful powres,
      Chirpe loud to thee out of their leavy cages
And thee their mother call to coole their kindly rages.

Then doe the savage beasts begin to play
    Their pleasant friskes, and loath their wonted food;

13

The Lyons rore; the Tygres loudly bray;
  The raging Buls rebellow through the wood,
  And breaking forth dare tempt the deepest flood
    To come where thou doest draw them with desire:
  So all things else, that nourish vitall blood,
    Soone as with fury thou doest them inspire
In generation seeke to quench their inward fire.

So all the world by thee at first was made,
  And dayly yet thou doest the same repayre:
Ne ought on earth that merry is and glad,
  Ne ought on earth that lovely is and fayre
  But thou the same for pleasure didst prepayre.
    Thou art the root of all that joyous is:
    Great God of men and women, queene of th'ayre,
    Mother of laughter and welspring of blisse,
O graunt that of my love at last I may not misse!

CATULLUS

CARMEN III

Cupids and Graces, mourn with me –
Men, too, of sensibility:
Gone is my darling's sparrow, gone
The sparrow that she doted on.

She loved him more than her own eyes,
For he, sweet thing, would recognise
His mistress as a maid her mother,
Nor leave her lap for any other,
But hither alight and thither spring,
In her sole service chirruping.

And now the shadow-glimmering track
He goes, whence none – they say – come back.

Ill tide you, dark and evil power,
You, that all prettiness devour –
So pretty a sparrow have you torn
Away, O cruel, for us to mourn.
Poor bird, for you my darling cries,
All red, and big with tears, her eyes.

CARMEN V

My sweetest Lesbia let us live and love,
And though the sager sort our deedes reprove,
Let us not way them: heav'ns great lampes doe dive
Into their west, and strait againe revive,
But soone as once set is our little light,
Then must we sleepe one ever-during night.

If all would lead their lives in love like mee,
Then bloudie swords and armour should not be,
No drum nor trumpet peaceful sleepes should move,
Unles alar'me came from the campe of love:
But fooles do live, and wast their little light,
And seeke with paine their ever-during night.

When timely death my life and fortune ends,
Let not my hearse be vext with mourning friends,
But let all lovers rich in triumph come,
And with sweet pastimes grace my happie tombe;
And Lesbia close up thou my little light,
And crowne with love my ever-during night.

CARMEN V

Come and let us live, my Dear,
Let us love and never fear
What the sourest Fathers say:
Brightest Sol that dies to-day
Lives again as blithe to-morrow;
But if we dark sons of sorrow
Set, O then how long a night
Shuts the eyes of our short light!
Then let amorous kisses dwell
On our lips, begin and tell
A thousand, and a hundred score,
An hundred, and a thousand more,
Till another thousand smother
That, and that wipe off another.
Thus at last when we have numbered
Many a thousand, many a hundred,
We'll confound the reckoning quite,
And lose our selves in wild delight:
While our joys so multiply
As shall mock the envious eye.

RICHARD CRASHAW

CARMEN VII

Nay, Lesbia, never ask me this,
How many Kisses will suffice?
Faith, 'tis a question hard to tell,
Exceeding hard; for you as well
May ask what sums of Gold suffice
The greedy Miser's boundless Wish:
Think what drops the Ocean store,
With all the Sands, that make its Shore:
Think what Spangles deck the Skies,
When Heaven looks with all its Eyes:
Or think how many Atoms came
To compose this mighty Frame:
Let all these the Counters be,
To tell how oft I'm kiss'd by thee:
Till no malicious Spy can guess
To what vast height the Scores arise;
Till weak Arithmetick grow scant,
And numbers for thy reck'ning want:
All these will hardly be enough
For me stark staring mad with Love.

CARMEN VIII

Harden now thy tyred hart, with more then flinty rage;
Ne'er let her false teares henceforth thy constant griefe
    asswage.
Once true happy dayes thou saw'st when shee stood
    firme and kinde,
Both as one then liv'd and held one eare, one tongue,
    one minde:
Not now those bright houres be fled, and ever
    may returne;
What then remaines but her untruths to mourne?

Silly Traytresse, who shall now thy carelesse
    tresses place?
Who thy pretty talke supply, whose eare thy
    musicke grace?
Who shall thy bright eyes admire? what lips triumph
    with thine?
Day by day who'll visit thee and say 'th'art
    onely mine'?
Such a time there was, God wot, but such
    shall never be:
Too oft, I feare, thou wilt remember me.

CARMEN XV

Aurelius, I'm entrusting you with all
I love most, with my boy. I ask a small
Favour. If you have ever pledged your soul
To keep some cherished object pure and whole,
Then guard him – I don't mean from any stranger
Walking the streets on business bent: the danger
I fear is you yourself and that great spike
That ruins good and naughty boys alike.
When you're outside the house, wave your erection
At any one you like, in what direction
You please, but (I'm not asking much, I trust)
Make him the one exception. If, though, lust
And sheer perversity unhinge your reason
And drive you to the abominable treason
Of plotting against me, a grisly fate
Awaits you. Feet chained, through the open gate
Of your own flesh you'll suffer, for your sins,
The thrust of radishes and mullets' fins.

CARMEN XXXI

Little gem of all-but-islands and of islands, Sirmio,
Whether set in landlocked waters, or in Ocean's
     freer flow –
Oh the pleasant seeing of thee, bright as ever –
     there below –
Far behind me, to the Northward, lie the dreamy
     lands of snow.
Oh the hour of mad rejoicing, oh the sweet good-bye
     to woe
As with quiet soul aweary of world-wandering
     to and fro
In we hurry through the doorway of our home of
     long ago . . .
Hail then, hail! Thy master welcome, welcome him,
     sweet Sirmio,
Leap for joy, ye tumbling waters, winking at the
     summer's glow,
Gaily through the house resounding let the peals of
     laughter go.

CARMEN XXXVI

Volusius' *Annals*, sheets for wiping
Bums with, come, pay my girl's vow. Both
Venus and Cupid heard her oath:
That if I lovingly returned
And stopped my fierce satiric sniping
She'd offer the lame god the worst
Poet's worst verses to be burned
With wood from trees that are accursed.
The worst of girls thought it amusing
To vow 'the worst' and do the choosing!
Now, goddess born of the blue brine,
Worshipped in all your holy places –
Idalium, Urii's open spaces,
Reed-rustling Cnidus, Golgi's shrine,
Ancon and Amathus and that town
That drinks the Adriatic trade,
Dyrrachium – if you think the joke
A neat and witty one, then mark down
Her vow as fair and squarely paid.
In the meantime, up you go in smoke,
Volusian *Annals*, paper fit
For bores and boors – and wiping shit!

CARMEN XLII

Hendecasyllables, help! Come to my call,
Rally from every quarter, all of you, all
The hendecasyllables there are! For, thinking
That she can make a fool of me, that stinking
Bitch has refused to give my notebooks back —
Can you believe it? Come with me, let's track
Her down and ask for them. 'Which girl?' you say.
Over there, that one. Look at the vulgar way
She struts the sidewalk like a second-rate
Comedienne, guffawing with that great
Gash of a mouth like a Cisalpine hound.
Hem her in! Claim our property! Standing round,
Chant, 'Rotten bitch, give back the notebooks which
You snitched! Give back the notebooks, rotten bitch!'
She doesn't care a damn? Right. 'Scum, filth, whore!'
Or anything else that we can think of more

Insulting still. No answer? Well, although
We've done our best, clearly we'll have to go
On trying. Since all else has failed, at least
Let's force a blush out of the brazen beast.
The chorus once more – this time raise the pitch:
'You rotten bitch, give back the notebooks which
You snitched. Give back the notebooks, rooten bitch!'
We're getting nowhere. She won't bat an eye.
To make some headway, we shall have to try
A new line, switch the method of attack:
Say, 'Pure, sweet lady, please *do* give them back.'

CARMEN XLV

Whil'st on Septimius panting Brest,
(Meaning nothing less than rest)
Acme lean'd her loving Head,
Thus the pleas'd Septimius said,
My dearest Acme, if I be
Once alive and love not thee
With a Passion far above
All that e're was called Love,
In Lybian Desart may
I become some Lions Prey,
Let him, Acme, let him tear
My Breast, when Acme is not there.

The God of Love who stood to hear him,
(The God of Love was always near him)
Pleas'd and tickl'd with the sound,
Sneez'd aloud, and all around
The little Loves that waited by,
Bow'd and blest the Augury.
Acme inflam'd with what he said,
Rear'd her gentle-bending head,
And her Purple Mouth with joy
Stretching to the delicious Boy
Twice (and twice could scarce suffice)
She kist his drunken rowling Eyes.

My little Life, my All (said she)
So may we ever Servents be
To this best God, and ne'er retain
Our hated Liberty again:
So may thy passion last for me,
As I a passion have for thee,
Greater and fiercer much than can
Be conceiv'd by thee a Man.

Into my Marrow it is gone,
Fixt and setled in the bone,
It reigns not only in my heart
But runs lik Life through ev'ry part.

She spoke; the God of Love aloud,
Sneez'd again, and all the croud
Of little Loves that waited by,
Bow'd and blest the Augury.

This good Omen thus from Heaven
Like a happy signal given,
Their Loves and Lives (all four) embrace,
And hand in hand run all the race,
To poor Septimius (who did now
Nothing else but Acme grow)
Acme's bosom was alone,
The whole Worlds Imperial Throne,

And to faithful Acme's mind
Septimius was all Human kind.

If the Gods would please to be
But advis'd for once by me,
I'd advise 'em when they spy
Any illustrious Piety,
To reward Her, if it be She;
To reward Him, if it be He;
With such a Husband, such a Wife,
With Acme's and Septimius's life.

CARMEN LI

Equal to Jove that youth must be –
Greater than Jove he seems to me –
Who, free from Jealousy's alarms,
Securely views thy matchless charms.
That cheek, which ever dimpling glows,
That mouth, from whence such music flows,
To him, alike, are always known,
Reserved for him, and him alone.
Ah! Lesbia! though 'tis death to me,
I cannot choose but look on thee;
But, at the sight, my senses fly;
I needs must gaze, but, gazing, die;
Whilst trembling with a thousand fears,
Parch'd to the throat my tongue adheres,
My pulse beats quick, my breath heaves short,
My limbs deny their slight support,
Cold dews my pallid face o'erspread,
With deadly languor droops my head,
My ears with tingling echoes ring,
And life itself is on the wing;
My eyes refuse the cheering light,
Their orbs are veil'd in starless night:
Such pangs my nature sinks beneath,
And feels a temporary death.

CARMEN LVI

Cato, it's ludicrous, too absurd!
Do listen, it's worth chuckling over.
If you hold Catullus in affection,
Laugh, Cato, for what's just occurred
Is the funniest thing you've ever heard.
I caught a tender little lover,
Bottom up, rogering his bird,
And, brandishing my own erection
(Venus forgive me!), made a third.

CARMEN LXX

My Mistresse sayes she'll marry none but me,
No not if Jove himself a Suitor be:
She sayes so; but what women say to kind
Lovers, we write in rapid streams and wind.

CARMEN XCII

I

Each Moment of the long-liv'd Day,
Lesbia for me does backward pray,
   And rails at me sincerely;
Yet I dare pawn my Life, my Eyes,
   My Soul, and all that Mortals prize,
That Lesbia loves me dearly.

II

Why shou'd you thus conclude, you'll say,
Faith 'tis my own beloved Way,
   And thus I hourly prove her;
Yet let me all those Curses share
That Heav'n can give, or Man can bear,
   If I don't strangely love her.

TOM BROWN

CARMEN XCII

Lesbia for ever on me rails;
　To talk on me she never fails:
Yet, hang me, but for all her Art;
　I find that I have gain'd her Heart:
My proof is thus: I plainly see
　The Case is just the same with me:
I curse her ev'ry hour sincerely;
　Yet, hang me, but I love her dearly.

CARMEN CI

By many lands and over many a wave
I come, my brother, to your piteous grave,
To bring you the last offering in death
And o'er dumb dust expend an idle breath;
For fate has torn your living self from me,
And snatched you, brother, O, how cruelly!
Yet take these gifts, brought as our fathers bade
For sorrow's tribute to the passing shade;
A brother's tears have wet them o'er and o'er;
And so, my brother, hail, and farewell evermore!

VIRGIL

From AENEID IV

Then doth unhappy Dido, given ore
   By her last hope, desire to die. The light
   Is irksom to her eys. To confirm more
   Her purpose to imbrace eternal night,
   Placing on th' Incense-burning Altars bright
   Her gifts, the holy water she beheld
   Converted to black ink (portentous sight!)
   And the pour'd wine to roaping blood congeal'd;
This thing to none, not to her sister, she reveal'd.

A Marble Fane too in the house she had
   Where lay her first Lords ashes, kept among
   Her most adored Reliques; 'twas with sad
   Dark Yew-tree, and the whitest fleeces hung.
   Hence in the night she heard her husbands tongue,
   Call her, she thought. And oft the boading Owl
   Alone on the house top harsh dirges sung,
   And with long noats quav'rd a doleful howl,
Besides old Prophesies, which terrifie her soul.

Cruel Æneas ev'n her sleeps torments:
   And still she dreams she's wandring all alone
   Through a long way with steep and dark descents,
   Calling her Tyrians in a Land, where none,
   But some pain'd Ghost Eccho's her with a groane.

As when mad Pentheus troops of Furies fright,
  Who sees a twofold Thebes, and double Sunne:
  Or when Orestes flyes his Mothers sight,
Hunting his bloody track with Hel-hounds by
      torchlight.

Sunke then with grief, possest with furies, bent
  On death, she plots the meanes, and in her Eye
  A feign'd hope springing, hiding her intent
  Accosts sad Anne. Partake thy sisters Joy,
  I've found a way to make him burne as I,
  Or turne me cold like him. Neere Phœbus set
  At the lands end doth Æthiopia lye,
  Where on great Atlas necke, the Heav'n thick set
With glorious Diamond-starres hangs like a Carkanet.

Of a great Sorceresse I have been told
  There borne, who did th' Hesperian Temple keepe,
  The Dragon fed, and sacred fruit of Gold
  Watcht on the tree which she for dew did steepe
  In Honey, and moist Poppy causing sleepe.
  Shee undertakes to cure the Love-sick breast,
  And whom shee list to plunge in Love as deepe,
  The waters course in Rivers to arrest,
And call down stars from Heav'n, and cal up ghosts
      from rest.

Under her tread thou shalt perceive Earth groane,
   And Oakes skip from the hills; I sweare to thee
   (Calling the Gods to record, and thine own
   Sweet head) that forc't to these black Arts I flee.
   Thou on some Tow'r a stack build secretly,
   Lay on it the mans cloathes, and sword which lyes
   Within, and, that which prov'd a grave to me,
   My Wedding Bed. So doth the Witch advise,
Ev'n that I blot out all the traytors memories.

This said, grew pale. Yet thinks not Anne that shee
   With these new Rites her funerall doth shade,
   Nor fears such Monsters, or worse extasie
   Then at Sycheus death; Therefore obay'd.
   But Dido, a great Pile of wood being made
   The place with flowr's and fatäl Cypresse crown'd,
   Thereon his cloathes and sword bequeathed laid,
   His Picture on the Bed, the mystick ground
Known only to her selfe. Altars are placed round.

With haire dispread like a black falling storme,
   Th'Inchantress thunders out three hundred names,
   Orchus, and Chaos, Hecate-triforme,
   Which Virgin Dian's triple-pow'r enseames,
   She sprinkled, too, Avernus fabulous streames:
   And hearts were sought for, sprouting forth ripe
     Bane,

With brazen sickles, cropt in the Moones beames,
And puld from new born Colt, that lumpe, which,
   ta'ne
From the Dams mouth, no love t'her issue doth remain.

Her self in a loose vest, one foot unshod,
   With meale in pious hands neer th' Altar drew,
   Witnesse ye guilty starres and every God
   (Saith she) I'm forc't to dye. Invokes them too
   Who care of Lovers take (if any doe)
   Unequally. 'Twas night, and conqu'ring sleepe,
   With weari'd bodies the whole earth did strew;
   When woods are quiet, and the cruell deep
When stars are half way down, when fields stil
   silence keep,

And beasts and painted Birds, which liquid Springs
   Inhabit, or which bushy Lands containe,
   Nuzling their cares beneath sleepes downy wings,
   Do bury the past dayes forgotten paine;
   All but the haplesse Queen, she doth refraine
   From rest, nor takes it at her eyes or heart.
   After long seeming dead, Love rose againe
   And fought with wrath, as when two Tydes
      do thwart,
Whilst thus her big thoughts roll & wallow to
   each part.

What shall I do? Shall I a suiter be
    To my old suitors, scorned by the new,
    And wooe those Kings so oft despis'd by me?
    What then? Shall I the Ilian Fleet pursue,
    And share all this mans fates? Yes, he doth shew
    Such sence of my first aides: Or say I wou'd,
    Whom he hath mockt, will not his proud ships too
    Reject? Ah foole, by whom the perjur'd brood
Of false Laomedon is not yet understood!

Grant they'd admit me, shall I flye alone
    With Mariners? Or chace him with the power
    Oth' emptyed Towne, and servants of mine own,
    And whom I scare from Tyre by the roots up tore,
    Compell to plough the horrid Seas once more?
    No, dye as thou deserv'st, cure woes with woe.
    Thou syster, first, when I my teares did showre
    To quench these rising flames, thou dids't
        them blow,
And out of cruel pity soldst me to the Foe.

Why might not I (alas) have mourn'd away
    My widdow'd youth as well as Turtles do?
    Nor twice have made my self misfortunes prey,
    Or to Sicheus ashes prov'd untrue?
    These words with sighs out of her bosome flew.
    Æneas slept aboord, all things prepared.

43

To whom again Joves sonne with the same hiew
    Divine, so silver-voyc'd, so golden hayr'd,
So straight and lovely shap't, thus rowsing him
    appear'd.

O Goddesse born, now dost thou sleepe? nor know
    How many dangers watch to compasse thee?
    Nor hear this good wind whispering thee to go?
    Purpos'd to dye, great plots and dire broods she,
    Who boyles with rage like a high going Sea.
    Flye whilst thous maist flye. If the morning finde
    Thee napping here, the Sea will cover'd be
    With Ships, the shoare with flames: Fly with
        the wind,
Trust that, but do not trust a womans fickle mind.

This said, he mixt himself with night: But then
    Æneas at these visions sore agast,
    Starts out of sleepe, and cryes, up, up, O men,
    Hoyse up your Sayles, flye to your Oares, row fast;
    Behold a God from Heav'n again bids haste,
    Cutting the wreathed Cable. O, who ere
    We follow thee, obey'd as late thou wast
    Most gladly. Aide what thou commandst, and steere
With prosp'rous stars bespoke as thou fly'st through
    their sphere.

This said, whipt out his Lightning Sword, and strooke
    The fastning ropes. Like zeale his patterne bred
    In all. They snatcht, they ran, the shoares for sook,
    Their Sayles like wings over the waves were spread;
    They comb'd with Oares gray Neptunes curled head.
    And now Aurora scattered rosie light
    Upon the Earth from Tythons purple bed.
    Whom Dido, having scoured all the night,
Discover'd from the Watch-Tower by her Ensignes
      white.

From AENEID VI

By a bláck lake protécted
And glóomy woods róund,
There gáped with a vást
Awful yáwn a deep cávern
All rúgged with shíngle,
Over which without hárm
Could no flýing thing páss,
Such a stéam from its dárk jaws
Exháled to heaven's cónvex;
For which réason the Gráïï
The pláce called Avérnus.

   Hére first the príestess
Sets fóur black steers stánding,
Ánd on their fóreheads
Póurs the wine sídeways;
And plúcking the úppermost
Háirs 'twixt the hórns,
Pláces the fírstlings
On the fíre of the áltar,
And alóud calls on Hécate
In Érebus poténtial
As wéll as in héaven.
And óthers the júgulars
Incíse from belów,

And in wíde, shallow sáucers
Recéive the warm blóod.
To the móther of the Fúries,
And tó her great síster,
Enéas himsélf slays
A fléecy, black lámb,
Ánd to thee, Próserpine,
A bárren-wombed héifer;
Then tó the king Stýgian
The níght altar ráises,
And an óx's whole cárcase
Upón its fire pláces,
And óver the hót roast
Póurs the fat óil.

But, behóld! at sunríse
The ground únder their féet
Is begínning to béllow,
And the móuntain tops wóody
To quáke to and fró,
Ánd through the dárkness
Dog-bítches are hówling;
For the Góddess is cóming: —

'Off! óff! ye profáne ones,'
The próphetess críes:
'Let not óne of you ánywhere

Ín the grove línger –
But thóu, draw thy swórd,
And set óut on thy róad;
For cóurage, Enéas,
Now, nów is the tíme;
For fírmness the tíme 's now.'
These wórds having úttered,
She plúnged all infúriate
Ínto the cáve's mouth;
Hé, with no timid step,
Kept páce with his guíde.

Ye Góds who rule óver
The émpire of spírits,
And yé, silent Shádes,
Ye, Cháos and Phlégethon,
Régions of wíde-brooding
Stíllness and níght,
Be the prívilege allówed me
To téll what I've héard,
Your sánction accórded
The thíngs to revéal
That in dárkness are súnk
And the dépths of the éarth.

In the lónely night, dárkling,
They wént through the sháde,

Through the réalms unsubstántial
And mánsions of Dis,
As one trável in the wóods
By the créscent moon's twílight,
When Júpiter plúnges
The ský into shádow,
And múrky night stríps
The wórld of its cólour.

In the véstibule's frónt,
And the véry begínning
And jáw's edge of Órcus,
Remórse has her cóuch placed
With Sórrow besíde her,
And thére pale Diséases
And sád Old Age dwéll,
And Pénury vile,
And ill-cóunselling Húnger,
And Féar, Death and Tóil,
Frightful fórms to behóld,
And, Déath's cousin, Sléep,
And the críminal Pássions;
And in frónt, as thou énterest,
Déath-dealing Wárfare,
Ánd the Euménides'
Íron bedchámbers,
And Díscord insénsate,

With blóody band týing
The snákes of her háir.

In the midst an aged élm
Its wide-branching árms
Huge and shády spreads óut,
Under whóse every léaf,
Vain, incónsequent Dréams,
They sáy, have their dwélling
And néstle in clústers.
Many mónsters besídes
Of béastly forms várious
Abóut the doors kénnel;
Centaurs, Górgons, and Hárpies,
Half-mán half-fish Scýllas,
Hundred-hánded Briáreus,
Lerna's béast hissing hórrid,
Flame-bélching Chiméra,
And the thrée-bodied Sháde.

Here Enéas his swórd grasps,
In súdden alárm,
And presénts the drawn édge
To thém coming ónward,
And séems to be bént
(Were it nót for the wárning
His skílled comrade gíves him

That they're nóthing but thin
Unsubstántial souls flítting
Under sémblance of bódies)
To rúsh in upón them,
And, áll to no púrpose,
Cleave the shádows in súnder.

From hénce the road léads
Tó where Tartárean
Ácheron's wáters
In vást muddy whírlpool
Rísing belch óver
The whóle of their sánd and lees
Ínto Cocýtus.
A férryman hórrid
Has chárge of these wáters,
Charon, térribly squálid,
With eýes of flame stáring,
And gréat grisly béard
Uncáred on chin lýing,
And sórdid garb hánging
Tied óver his shóulder:
Althóugh somewhat áged,
The Gód is still hárdy,
And wéars his years wéll;
And himsélf with a lóng pole
The bóat forward scúlling,

Himsélf the sails ténding,
Acróss in his rústy craft
Férries his fréight.

  With a rúsh the whole crówd
Toward the férry was póuring;
Men and mátrons were thére,
And magnánimous héroes,
The tásk of life óver,
 And yóung lads and máidens,
And yóuths whom their párents
Saw ón the pile pláced;
As númerous as léaves fall
Detáched in the fórest,
In the first chill of áutumn;
Or as bírds from the hígh-deep
Tóward the land shóaling
When the cóld season róuts
And to súnny climes sénds them
Awáy beyond séa.

ECLOGUE II

For one fair face – his master's idol – burned
The shepherd Corydon; and hope had none.
Day after day he came ('twas all he could)
Where, piles of shadow, thick the beeches rose:
There, all alone, his unwrought phrases flung,
Bootless as passionate, to copse and crag.
'Hardhearted! Naught car'st thou for all my songs,
Naught pitiest. I shall die, one day, for thee.
The very cattle court cool shadows now,
Now the green lizard hides beneath the thorn:
And for the reaper, faint with driving heat,
The handmaids mix the garlic-salad strong.
My only mates, the crickets – as I track
'Neath the fierce sun thy steps – make shrill the woods.
Better to endure the passion and the pride
Of Amaryllis: better to endure

Menalcas – dark albeit as thou art fair.
Put not, oh fair, in difference of hue
Faith overmuch: the white May-blossoms drop
And die; the hyacinth swart, men gather it.
Thy scorn am I: thou ask'st not whence I am,
How rich in snowy flocks, how stored with milk.
O'er Sicily's green hills a thousand lambs
Wander, all mine: my new milk fails me not
In summer or in snow. Then I can sing
All songs Amphion the Dircæan sang,
Piping his flocks from Attic Aracynth.
Nor am I all uncouth. For yesterday,
When winds had laid the seas, I, from the shore,
Beheld my image. Little need I fear
Daphnis, though thou wert judge, or mirrors lie.
– Oh! be content to haunt ungentle fields,
A cottager, with me; bring down the stag,
And with green switch drive home thy flocks of kids:
Like mine, thy woodland songs shall rival Pan's!
– 'Twas Pan first taught us reed on reed to fit
With wax: Pan watches herd and herdsman too.
– Nor blush that reeds should chafe thy pretty lip.
What pains Amyntas took, this skill to gain!
I have a pipe – seven stalks of different lengths
Compose it – which Damœtas gave me once.
Dying he said, "At last 'tis all thine own."
The fool Amyntas heard, and grudged, the praise.

Two fawns moreover (perilous was the gorge
Down which I tracked them –!) – dappled still
        each skin –
Drain daily two ewe-udders; all for thee.
Long Thestylis has cried to make them hers.
Hers be they – since to thee my gifts are dross.

Be mine, oh fairest! See! for thee the Nymphs
Bear baskets lily-laden: Naiads bright
For thee crop poppy-crests and violets pale,
With daffodil and fragrant fennel-bloom:
Then, weaving casia in and all sweet things,
Soft hyacinth paint with yellow marigold.
Apples *I*'ll bring thee, hoar with tender bloom,
And chestnuts – which my Amaryllis loved,
And waxen plums: let plums too have their day.
And thee I'll pluck, oh bay, and, myrtle, thee
Its neighbour: neighboured thus your sweets shall mix.
– Pooh! Thou'rt a yokel, Corydon. Thy love
Laughs at thy gifts: if gifts must win the day,
Rich is Iolas. What thing have I,
Poor I, been asking – while the winds and boars
Ran riot in my pools and o'er my flowers?

– Yet, fool, whom fliest thou? Gods have dwelt in
        woods,
And Dardan Paris. Citadels let her

Who built them, Pallas, haunt: green woods for me.
Grim lions hunt the wolf, and wolves the kid,
And kids at play the clover-bloom. I hunt
Thee only: each one drawn to what he loves.
See! trailing from their necks the kine bring home
The plough, and, as he sinks, the sun draws out
To twice their length the shadows. Still I burn
With love. For what can end or alter love?

Thou'rt raving, simply raving, Corydon.
Clings to thy leafy elm thy half-pruned vine.
Why not begin, at least, to plait with twigs
And limber reeds some useful homely thing?
Thou'lt find another love, if scorned by this.'

ECLOGUE IV

Sicilian Muse, begin a loftier strain!
Though lowly shrubs and trees that shade the plain
Delight not all; Sicilian Muse, prepare
To make the vocal woods deserve a consul's care.
The last great age, foretold by sacred rhymes,
Renews its finish'd course; Saturnian times
Roll round again, and mighty years, begun
From their first orb, in radiant circles run.
The base degenerate iron offspring ends;
A golden progeny from heaven descends:
O chaste Lucina, speed the mother's pains,
And haste the glorious birth; thy own Apollo reigns!
The lovely boy, with his auspicious face,
Shall Pollio's consulship and triumph grace;
Majestic months set out with him to their appointed
      race.

The father banish'd virtue shall restore,
And crimes shall threat the guilty world no more.
The son shall lead the life of gods, and be
By gods and heroes seen, and gods and heroes see.
The jarring nations he in peace shall bind,
And with paternal virtues rule mankind.
Unbidden earth shall wreathing ivy bring
And fragrant herbs (the promises of spring)
As her first offerings to her infant king.
The goats, with strutting dugs, shall homeward speed,
And lowing herds secure from lions feed.
His cradle shall with rising flowers be crown'd;
The serpent's brood shall die: the sacred ground
Shall weeds and poisonous plants refuse to bear;
Each common bush shall Syrian roses wear.
But when heroic verse his youth shall raise
And form it to hereditary praise,
Unlabour'd harvests shall the fields adorn,
And cluster'd grapes shall blush on every thorn.
The knotted oaks shall showers of honey weep,
And through the matted grass the liquid gold
        shall creep.
Yet, of old fraud some footsteps shall remain,
The merchant still shall plough the deep for gain:
Great cities shall with walls be compass'd round;
And sharpen'd shares shall vex the fruitful ground,
Another Typhis shall new seas explore,

Another Argos land the chiefs upon the Iberian shore;
Another Helen other wars create,
And great Achilles urge the Trojan fate.
But when to ripen'd manhood he shall grow,
The greedy sailor shall the seas forego;
No keel shall cut the waves for foreign ware;
For every soil shall every product bear.
The labouring hind his oxen shall disjoin,
No plough shall hurt the glebe, no pruning-hook the vine,
Nor wool shall in dissembled colours shine.
But the luxurious father of the fold,
With native purple, or unborrow'd gold,
Beneath his pompous fleece shall proudly sweat;
And under Tyrian robes the lamb shall bleat.
The Fates, when they this happy web have spun,
Shall bless the sacred clue, and bid it smoothly run.
Mature in years, to ready honours move,
O of celestial seed! O foster-son of Jove!
See, labouring Nature calls thee to sustain
The nodding frame of heaven, and earth, and main;
See, to their base restor'd, earth, seas, and air,
And joyful ages from behind, in crowding ranks
          appear.
To sing thy praise, would heaven my breath prolong,
Infusing spirits worthy such a song,
Not Thracian Orpheus should transcend my lays,
Nor Linus, crown'd with never-fading bays, –

Though each his heavenly parent should inspire,
The Muse instruct the voice, and Phoebus tune
    the lyre.
Should Pan contend in verse, and thou my theme,
Arcadian judges should their God condemn.
Begin, auspicious boy, to cast about
Thy infant eyes, and with a smile thy mother
    single out;
Thy mother well deserves that short delight,
The nauseous qualms of ten long months and travail
    to requite.
Then smile; the frowning infant's doom is read,
No god shall crown the board, nor goddess bless
    the bed.

GEORGIC IV

Next I come to the manna, the heavenly gift of honey.
Look kindly on this part too, my friend. I'll tell of a tiny
Republic that makes a show well worth your
     admiration –
Great-hearted leaders, a whole nation whose work
     is planned,
Their morals, groups, defences – I'll tell you in due order.
A featherweight theme: but one that can load me with
     fame, if only
No wicked fairy cross me, and the Song-god come to
     my call.
   For a start you must find your bees a suitable home,
     a position
Sheltered from wind (for wind will stop them carrying
     home
Their forage), a close where sheep nor goats come
     butting in

To jump on the flowers, nor blundering heifer stray
    to flick
The dew from the meadow and stamp its springing
    grasses down.
Discourage the lizard, too, with his lapis-lazuli back.
From their rich folds, the bee-eater and other birds,
And the swallow whose breast was blooded once by a
    killer's hand:
For these wreak wholesale havoc, snap up your bees
    on the wing
And bear them off as a tit-bit for their ungentle
    nestlings.
But mind there's a bubbling spring nearby, a pool
    moss-bordered,
And a rill ghosting through the grass:
See, too, that a palm or tall oleaster shadow the entrance,
For thus, when the new queens lead out the earliest
    swarms –
The spring all theirs – and the young bees play, from
    hive unprisoned,
The bank may be handy to welcome them in out of
    the heat
And the tree meet them halfway and make them at
    home in its foliage.
Whether the water flows or is stagnant, fling in
    the middle
Willow boughs criss-cross and big stones,

That the bees may have plenty of bridges to stand on
    and dry their wings
At the summer sun, in case a shower has caught them
    loitering
Or a gust of east wind ducked them suddenly in
    the water.
Green spurge-laurel should grow round about,
    wild thyme that perfumes
The air, masses of savory rich-breathing, and
    violet beds
Sucking the channelled stream.
    Now for the hive itself. Remember, whether you
    make it
By stitching concave bark or weaving tough withies
    together,
To give it a narrow doorway: for winter grips and
    freezes
The honey, and summer's melting heat runs it off
    to waste.
Either extreme is feared by the bees. It is not for fun
That they're so keen on caulking with wax the
    draughty chinks
In their roof, and stuff the rim of their hive with
    flowery pollen,
Storing up for this very job a glue they have gathered
Stickier than bird-lime or pitch from Anatolia.
Often too, if reports are true, they dig deep shelters

Underground and keep house there, or out of the way
    are found
In a sandstone hollow or the heart of a rotten tree.
None the less, you should smear with smooth mud
    their chinky chambers
Solicitously for warmth, and lay a thin dressing
    of leaves.
Don't have a yew too close to their house, or burn
    in a brazier
Reddening crab-shells: never risk them near a bog,
Or where there's a stink of mud, or a rock formation
    echoes
Hollow when struck and returns your voice like a
    ghostly reflection.
  For the rest, when the golden sun has driven winter
    to ground
And opened up all the leagues of the sky in summer
    light,
Over the glades and woodlands at once they love
    to wander
And suck the shining flowers and delicate sip the streams.
Sweet then is their strange delight
As they cherish their children, their nestlings:
    then with craftsmanship they
Hammer out the fresh wax and mould the tacky honey.
Then, as you watch the swarm bursting from hive and
    heavenward

Soaring, and floating there on the limpid air of summer –
A vague and wind-warped column of cloud to your
        wondering eyes: –
Notice them, how they always make for fresh water
        and leafy
Shelter. Here you shall sprinkle fragrances to
        their taste –
Crushed balm, honeywort humble –
Make a tinkling noise round about and clash the
        Mother-god's cymbals.
They will settle down of their own accord in the place
        you have perfumed,
And crawl to the innermost room for rest, as their
        custom is.
For some are unkempt and squalid, like a traveller
        when he comes
Athirst off a dusty road and spits the grit from his
        dry mouth;
While others gleam and glitter,
Their bodies perfectly marked in a pattern of shining
        gold.
These are the better breed: from these at the right
        season
Sweet honey you'll get – not sweet so much as pure,
        and fit
To soften your wine's harsh flavour.
But when the swarms fly aimlessly and sport in the sky,

Looking down on their combs, leaving the hives to cool,
You must put a stop to this empty and irresponsible play.
It is not hard to stop.
Tear off the wings of their queens: while these wait on
     the ground,
No bee will dare to leave his base or take off for a flight.
Let gardens breathing a scent of yellow flowers allure
     them:
Let the god of gardens, who watches for birds and
     robbers, keep them
Safe with his hook of willow.
The bee-keeper for his part should fetch down thyme
     and pine
From the hills above, and plant them broadly around
     the bees' home:
His hands should grow work-hardened, bedding the
     soil with fertile
Shoots, watering them well.
   Indeed, were it not that already my work has made
     its landfall
And I shorten sail and eagerly steer for the harbour
     mouth,
I'd sing perhaps of rich gardens, their planning and
     cultivation,
The rose beds of Paestum that blossom twice in a year,
The way endive rejoices to drink from a rivulet,
The bank all green with celery, the cucumber snaking

Amid the grass and swelling to greatness: I'd not
    forget
Late-flowering narcissus or gum-arabic's ringlet
    shoots,
Pale ivy, shore-loving myrtle.
I remember once beneath the battlements of Oebalia,
Where dark Galaesus waters the golden fields of corn,
I saw an old man, a Corycian, who owned a few poor
    acres
Of land once derelict, useless for arable,
No good for grazing, unfit for the cultivation of vines.
But he laid out a kitchen garden in rows amid the
    brushwood,
Bordering it with white lilies, verbena, small-seeded
    poppy.
He was happy there as a king. He could go indoors
    at night
To a table heaped with dainties he never had to buy.
His the first rose of spring, the earliest apples in autumn:
And when grim winter still was splitting the rocks
    with cold
And holding the watercourses with curb of ice, already
That man would be cutting his soft-haired hyacinths,
    complaining
Of summer's backwardness and the west winds slow
    to come.
His bees were the first to breed,

Enriching him with huge swarms: he squeezed the
     frothy honey
Before anyone else from the combs: he had limes and a
     wealth of pine trees:
And all the early blossom, that clothed his trees with
     promise
Of an apple crop, by autumn had come to maturity.
He had a gift, too, for transplanting in rows the far-
     grown elm,
The hardwood pear, the blackthorn bearing its weight
     of sloes,
And the plane that already offered a pleasant shade
     for drinking.
   So, to compare small things
With great, an inborn love of possession impels the
     bees
Each to his own office. The old are the town's wardens,
Who wall the honeycombs and frame the intricate
     houses.
Tired, as the night deepens, the young return from
     labour,
Their legs laden with thyme: they feed afar on
     the arbute,
The silvery willow, the spurge laurel, the fire-blush
     saffron,
The lime blossom so rich, the rust-red martagon lily.
For one and all one work-time, and a like rest from work.

At morning they hurry from the hives, all helter-
      skelter: again,
When the Evening Star has told them to leave their
      meadow pasture,
They make for home, they refresh themselves. What
      a murmuring
You hear as they drone around their policies and
      doorsteps!
Later, they settle down in their cells for the night,
      a silence
Falls, a drowsy fatigue falls.
If rain threatens, be sure they'll not roam too far afield
From their hives: they mistrust the sky, should an east
      wind be due:
At such times safely beneath the walls of their town
      they forage
Around, making brief excursions, and often carry
      some ballast,
As dinghies do to stiffen them in a high sea – they lift
Wee stones, and with these they weather the cloud-
      tossed solitudes.
   If ever you wish to unseal the treasure-vaults of their
      palace
Where the honey's hoarded, first sprinkle yourself
      with water,
Rinse your mouth, and release a smoke to chivvy
      them out.

Twice a year men gather their harvest and heavy
　　produce: —
As soon as Taÿgete the Pleiad has turned her
　　handsome
Face to the earth and spurned with her foot the
　　repulsed ocean;
Or again when, fleeing the star of the rainy Fish,
　　she goes
Gloomily down the sky and is drowned in a winter sea.
Unbounded then is the rage of the bees, provoked they
　　breathe
Venom into their stabs, they cling to your veins
　　and bury
Their stings — oh yes, they put their whole souls into
　　the wound.
But if you fear a hard winter for them and wish to
　　provide for
The future, pitying their bruised spirits and bankrupt
　　estate,
Even then you should trouble to fumigate with thyme
And cut back the empty cells. For often the newt
　　unnoticed
Nibbles the combs, their cubicles are black with light-
　　shunning beetles,
And the drone gate-crashes their dinner:
There's the assassin hornet who, heavier armed
　　than they,

Attacks them: there's the sinister tribe of moths;
    and Minerva's
Bugbear, the spider, draping his slack nets over the
    doorway.
But the more exhausted the bees, the keener they'll
    be to mend
The wreck of their ruined state,
Restock the store-rooms and fashion the flowery
    granaries.
  Since life brings to the bees the same bad luck as
    to humans,
They may suffer severe illness –
An epidemic you'll know by certain definite signs.
The sick change colour at once, and their faces are
    deformed
By dreadful emaciation: the bodies of the dead
They carry out of doors and bear in a sad cortège:
With clutching feet they hang
From the doorway, or moon about within their closed
    mansion
Listless with hunger all, numbed by a cramping cold.
Then there is heard a deeper sound, a hum sustained
As when a chill south wind murmurs among woods
Or the waves of a troubled sea moan and hiss at the
    ebb-tide
Or fierce flames roar heaving behind a furnace door.
I recommend here that you burn the pungent galbanum,

And instil honey through pipes of reed, going out of
    your way
To coax the invalid creatures back to familiar food.
It's a good thing also to add the juice of pounded oak-
    apples,
And dried rose-leaves, or wine boiled rich over a
    strong fire,
Raisins from the Psythian vine,
Thyme of Attica, and centaury strong-smelling.
There's a flower of the meadow, too, that our farmers
    call 'amellus':
It's easy enough to find,
For it raises up from a single stool a forest of stems;
Golden the disk, raying out into petals whose dark
    violet
Is shot with a purple shine:
Often the gods' altars are adorned with garlands of it:
Its taste is rough to the tongue: shepherds gather it on
    the close-cropped
Valley slopes and beside the meandering stream of
    Mella.
Boil the roots of this flower in fragrant wine, and serve it
In basketfuls at their door, a tonic food for the bees.

HORACE

ODES I, 5

What slender Youth bedew'd with liquid odours
Courts thee on Roses in some pleasant Cave,
   Pyrrha for whom bindst thou
   In wreaths thy golden Hair,
Plain in thy neatness; O how oft shall he
On Faith and changèd Gods complain: and Seas
   Rough with black winds and storms
   Unwonted shall admire:
Who now enjoyes thee credulous, all Gold,
Who always vacant always amiable
   Hopes thee; of flattering gales
   Unmindfull. Hapless they
To whom thou untry'd seem'st fair. Me in my vow'd
Picture the sacred wall declares t' have hung
   My dank and dropping weeds
   To the stern God of Sea.

ODES I, 5

What Stripling now Thee discomposes,
In Woodbine Rooms, on Beds of Roses,
 For whom thy Auburn Haire
 Is spread, Unpainted Faire?
How will he one day curse thy Oaths
And Heav'n that witness'd your Betroaths!
 How will the poor Cuckold,
 That deems thee perfect Gold,
Bearing no stamp but his, be mas'd
To see a suddain Tempest rais'd!
 He dreams not of the Windes,
 And thinks all Gold that shines.
For me my Votive Table showes
That I have hung up my wet Clothes
 Upon the Temple Wall
 Of Seas great Admirall.

ODES I, 5

What mean those Amorous Curles of Jet?
   For what heart-Ravisht Maid
Dost thou thy Hair in order set,
   Thy Wanton Tresses Braid?
And thy vast Store of Beauties open lay,
That she deluded Fancy leads astray.

For pitty hide thy Starry eyes,
   Whose Languishments destroy:
And look not on the Slave that dyes
   With an Excess of Joy.
Defend thy Coral Lips, thy Amber Breath;
To taste these Sweets lets in a Certain Death.

Forbear, fond Charming Youth, forbear,
   Thy words of Melting Love:
Thy Eyes thy Language well may spare
   One Dart enough can move.
And she that hears thy voice and sees thy Eyes
With too much Pleasure, too much Softness dies.

Cease, Cease, with Sighs to warm my Soul,
   Or press me with thy Hand:
Who can the kindling fire controul,
   The tender force withstand?
Thy Sighs and Touches like wing'd Lightning fly,
And are the God of Loves Artillery.

APHRA BEHN   77

ODES I, 9

One dazzling mass of solid snow
   Soracte stands; the bent woods fret
   Beneath their load; and, sharpest-set
With frost, the streams have ceased to flow.

Pile on great faggots and break up
   The ice: let influence more benign
   Enter with four-years-treasured wine,
Fetched in the ponderous Sabine cup:

Leave to the Gods all else. When they
   Have once bid rest the winds that war
   Over the passionate seas, no more
Grey ash and cypress rock and sway.

Ask not what future suns shall bring:
    Count to-day gain, whate'er it chance
    To be: nor, young man, scorn the dance
Nor deem sweet love an idle thing,

Ere Time thy April youth hath changed
    To sourness. Park and public walk
    Attract thee now, and whispered talk
At twilight meetings pre-arranged;

Hear now the pretty laugh that tells
    In what dim corner lurks thy love;
    And snatch a bracelet or a glove
From wrist or hand that scarce rebels.

C. S. CALVERLEY   79

ODES I, 9

Be patient, friend, nor seek to know
What length of years be still to go
    For you, for me; nor search the lines
    Of eastern horoscopes for signs
That such forbidden numbers show.

Accept as such this life below,
And, should these bitter winds that blow
    Mark the last sun for us that shines,
        Be patient, friend.

E'en as we chat, our jealous foe,
Time flies ahead, alas, not slow;
    A little space our term confines.
    Enjoy to-day, decant your wines,
Herein true wisdom lies, and so
        Be patient, friend.

ODES I, 11

Seek not, for thou shalt not find it, what my end,
    what thine shall be;
Ask not of Chaldaea's science what God wills,
    Leuconöe:
Better far, what comes, to bear it. Haply many a
    wintry blast
Waits thee still; and this, it may be, Jove ordains
    to be thy last,
Which flings now the flagging sea-wave on the
    obstinate sandstone-reef.
Be thou wise: fill up the wine-cup; shortening,
    since the time is brief,
Hopes that reach into the future. While I speak,
    hath stol'n away
Jealous Time. Mistrust To-morrow, catch the
    blossom of To-day.

C. S. CALVERLEY

ODES I, 22

Virtue, Dear Friend, needs no Defence,
The surest Guard is Innocence:
None knew, till Guilt created Fear,
What darts or poyson'd Arrows were.

Integrity undaunted goes
Through Lybian Sands or Scythian Snows,
Or where Hydaspes wealthy side
Pays Tribute to the Persian Pride.

For as (by amorous Thoughts betray'd)
Careless in Sabine Woods I stray'd,
A grisly foaming Wolf, unfed,
Met me unarm'd, yet trembling fled.

No Beast of more portentous Size,
In the Hercinian Forest lies;
None fiercer, in Numidia bred,
With Carthage were in Triumph led.

Set me in the Remotest Place,
That Neptune's frozen Arms embrace,
Where angry Jove did never spare
One Breath of kind and temp'rate Air:

Set me, where on some pathless Plain
The swarthy Africans complain,
To see the Char'ot of the Sun
So near the scorching Country run:

The burning Zone, the Frozen Isles,
Shall hear me sing of Cælia's Smiles,
All Cold but in her Breast I will despise,
And dare all Heat but that of Cælia's Eyes.

ODES I, 23

Why, whenever she can spy me,
Like a fawn will Chloe fly me?
Like a fawn, its mother seeking
O'er the hills, through brambles breaking;
Frightened if the breezes move
But a leaflet in the grove;
Or a branch the Zephyr tosses;
Or its path a lizard crosses;
Nothing can its fears dissemble –
Heart and knees together tremble.
Stop, my love; thou needst not fear me,
For I follow not to tear thee
Like the lion, prowling o'er
Far Getulia's savage shore:
Stop – thy budding charms discover
'Tis thy time to choose a lover.

ODES I, 25

The bloods and bucks of this lewd town
    No longer shake your windows down
        With knocking;
Your door stands still, no more you hear
'I die for you, O Lydia dear',
        Love's God your slumbers rocking.

Forsaken, in some narrow lane
    You in your turn will loud complain,
        Gallants no more engaging:
Whilst north-winds roar, and lust, whose pow'r
Makes madding mares the meadows scour,
        Is in your bosom raging.

You're griev'd, and quite eat up with spleen,
    That ivy and sweet myrtle green
        Young men alone long after;
And that away they dri'd leaves throw,
And let them down the river go
        With laughter.

ODES I, 38

Ah child, no Persian – perfect art!
Crowns composite and braided bast
They tease me. Never know the part
    Where roses linger last.

Bring natural myrtle, and have done:
Myrtle will suit your place and mine:
And set the glasses from the sun
    Beneath the tackled vine.

G. M. HOPKINS

Boy, I hate their empty shows;
   Persian garlands I detest;
Bring not me the late-blown rose,
   Lingering after all the rest.

Plainer myrtle pleases me,
   Thus outstretch'd beneath my vine;
Myrtle more becoming thee,
   Waiting with thy master's wine.

ODES II, 4

O Phoceus, think it no disgrace
    To love your maid, since Thetis heir,
Tho' proud, of old was in your case,
      Briseis was so fair.
– The slave Tecmessa at her feet
    Saw her lord Ajax – Atreus son
Lov'd his fair captive in the heat
      Of conquest, that he won,
When beat by that Thessalian boy,
    The Phrygian host was disarray'd,
And Hector's death, the fall of Troy,
      An easy purchase made.
Who knows what wealth thou hast to claim,
    Rich parents may thy Phyllis grace,
Surely the Gods have been to blame
      To one of royal race.
You cannot think her meanly born,
    Nor worthless cou'd her mother be,
Whose heart has such ingenuous scorn
      For wealth, and love for thee.
Her face, her limbs so form'd t' engage,
    I praise with a safe conscience still –
Shun to suspect a man, whose age
      Is going down the hill.

CHRISTOPHER SMART   87

ODES II, 8

Did any punishment attend
    Thy former perjuries,
I should believe a second time
    Thy charming flatteries:
Did but one wrinkle mark this face,
Or hadst thou lost one single grace.

No sooner hast thou, with false vows,
    Provok'd the powers above
But thou art fairer than before,
    And we are more in love.
Thus Heaven and Earth seem to declare
They pardon falsehood in the fair.

Sure 'tis no crime vainly to swear
    By every power on high,
And call our buried mother's ghost
    A witness to the lie:
Heaven at such perjury connives,
And Venus, with a smile, forgives.

The Nymphs, and cruel Cupid too,
    Sharpening his pointed dart
On an old hone besmear'd with blood,
    Forbear thy perjur'd heart.
Fresh youth grows up to wear thy chains,
And the old slave no freedom gains.

Thee mothers for their eldest sons,
    Thee wretched misers fear,
Lest thy prevailing beauty should
    Seduce the hopeful heir;
New-married virgins fear thy charms
Should keep their bridegrooms from their arms.

SIR CHARLES SEDLEY

ODES II, 10

Receive, dear friend, the truths I teach,
So shalt thou live beyond the reach
  Of adverse fortune's power;
Not always tempt the distant deep,
Nor always timorously creep
  Along the treacherous shore.

He that holds fast the golden mean,
And lives contentedly between
  The little and the great,
Feels not the wants that pinch the poor,
Nor plagues that haunt the rich man's door,
  Imbittering all his state.

The tallest pines feel most the power
Of wintry blast, the loftiest tower
  Comes heaviest to the ground;
The bolts that spare the mountain's side,
His cloud-capt eminence divide
  And spread the ruin round.

The well-inform'd philosopher
Rejoices with a wholesome fear,
    And hopes in spite of pain;
If winter bellow from the north,
Soon the sweet spring comes dancing forth,
    And nature laughs again.

What if thine heaven be overcast?
The dark appearance will not last,
    Expect a brighter sky;
The God that strings the silver bow,
Awakes sometimes the Muses too,
    And lays his arrows by.

If hindrances obstruct thy way,
Thy magnanimity display,
    And let thy strength be seen;
But oh! if Fortune fill thy sail
With more than a propitious gale,
    Take half thy canvas in!

From ODES II, 14

His age, Dedicated to his peculiar friend,
M. John Wickes, under the name of Posthumus

Ah Posthumus! Our yeares hence flye,
And leave no sound; nor piety,
     Or prayers, or vow
Can keepe the wrinkle from the brow:
     But we must on,
As Fate do's lead or draw us; none,
None, Posthumus, co'd ere decline
The doome of cruell Proserpine.

The pleasing wife, the house, the ground
Must all be left, no one plant found
     To follow thee,
Save only the Curst-Cipresse tree:
     A merry mind
Looks forward, scornes what's left behind:
Let's live, my Wickes, then, while we may,
And here enjoy our Holiday.

W'ave seen the past-best Times, and these
Will nere return, we see the Seas,
     And Moons to wain;
But they fill up their Ebbs again:
     But vanisht man,

Like to a Lilly-lost, nere can,
Nere can repullulate, or bring
His dayes to see a second Spring.

But on we must, and thither tend,
Where Anchus and rich Tullus blend
        Their sacred seed:
Thus has Infernall Jove decreed;
        We must be made,
Ere long, a song, ere long, a shade.
Why then, since life to us is short,
Lets make it full up, by our sport.

Crown we our Heads with Roses then,
And 'noint with Tirian Balme; for when
        We two are dead,
The world with us is buried.
        Then live we free,
As is the Air, and let us be
Our own fair wind, and mark each one
Day with the white and Luckie stone.

From ODES III, 3

I

The man of firm, and noble soul,
No factious clamours can controul;
No threat'ning tyrant's darkling brow,
   Can swerve him from his just intent;
Gales the warring waves which plow,
   By Auster on the billows spent,
To curb the Adriatic main,
Would awe his fix'd determined mind in vain.

II

Aye, and the red right arm of Jove,
Hurtling his lightnings from above,
With all his terrors there unfurl'd,
   He would, unmov'd, unaw'd, behold;
The flames of an expiring world,
   Again in crashing chaos roll'd
In vast promiscuous ruin hurl'd,
Might light his glorious funeral pile,
Still dauntless midst the wreck of earth he'd smile.

ODES III, 7: *An imitation*

I

Dear Molly, why so oft in Tears?
Why all these Jealousies and Fears,
   For thy bold Son of Thunder?
Have Patience till we've conquer'd France,
Thy Closet shall be stor'd with Nants;
   Ye Ladies like such Plunder.

II

Before Toulon thy Yoke-mate lies,
Where all the live-long Night he sighs
   For thee in lowsy Cabbin:
And tho' the Captain's Chloe cries,
''Tis I, dear Bully, prithee rise –'
   He will not let the Drab in.

III

But she, the Cunning'st Jade alive,
Says, 'Tis the ready way to thrive,
   By sharing Female Bounties:
And, if he'll be but kind one Night,
She Vows, He shall be dubb'd a Knight,
   When she is made a Countess.

IV

Then tells of smooth young Pages whipp'd,
Cashier'd, and of their Liv'ries stripp'd,
   Who late to Peers belonging;
Are nightly now compell'd to trudge
With Links, because they would not drudge
   To save their Ladies Longing.

V

But Vol the Eunuch cannot be
A Colder Cavalier than he,
   In all such Love-Adventures:
Then pray do you, dear Molly, take
Some Christian Care, and do not break
   Your Conjugal Indentures.

VI

Bellair! Who does not Bellair know?
The Wit, the Beauty, and the Beau,
   Gives out, He loves you dearly:
And many a Nymph attack'd with Sighs,
And soft Impertinence and Noise,
   Full oft has beat a Parley.

VII

But, pretty Turtle, when the Blade
Shall come with am'rous Serenade,
   Soon from the Window rate him:
But if Reproof will not prevail,
And he perchance attempt to scale,
   Discharge the Jordan at him.

GEORGE STEPNEY

ODES III, 13

Blandusian Spring, than glass more brightly clear,
Worthy of flowers and dulcet wine,
To-morrow shall a kid be thine,
Whose brow, where the first budding horns appear,
Battles and loves portends – portends in vain,
For he shall pour his crimson blood
To stain, bright Spring, thy gelid flood,
Nor e'er shall seek the wanton herd again.
Thee Sirius smites not from his raging star;
Thy tempting gloom a cool repose
To many a vagrant herd bestows,
And to faint oxen weary of the share;
Thou too 'mid famous fountains shalt display
Thy glory while I sing the oak
That hangs above the hollow rock
Whence thy loquacious waters leap away.

ODES III, 16

I

A Tower of Brass, one would have said,
　　And Locks, and Bolts, and Iron bars,
And Guards, as strict as in the heat of wars,
Might have preserv'd one Innocent Maiden-head.
The jealous Father thought he well might spare,
　　　　All further jealous Care,
And as he walkt, t' himself alone he smil'd,
　　　To think how Venus Arts he had beguil'd;
　　　And when he slept, his rest was deep,
But Venus laugh'd to see and hear him sleep.
　　　She taught the Amorous Jove
　　　A Magical receit in Love,
Which arm'd him stronger, and which help'd him
　　　more,
Than all his Thunder did, and his Almighty-ship
　　　before.

II

She taught him Loves Elixar, by which Art,
His Godhead into Gold he did convert,
　　　No Guards did then his passage stay,
　　　He pass'd with ease; Gold was the Word;
Subtle as Lightning, bright and quick and fierce,
　　　Gold through Doors and Walls did pierce;

And as that works sometimes upon the sword,
      Melted the Maiden-head away,
Even in the secret scabbard where it lay.
      The prudent Macedonian King,
To blow up Towns, a Golden Mine did spring.
      He broke through Gates with this Petar,
'Tis the great Art of Peace, the Engine 'tis of War;
      And Fleets and Armies follow it afar,
The Ensign 'tis at Land, and 'tis the Seamans Star.

III

Let all the World, slave to this Tyrant be,
Creature to this Disguised Deitie,
      Yet it shall never conquer me.
A Guard of Virtues will not let it pass,
And wisdom is a Tower of stronger brass.
The Muses Lawrel round my Temples spread,
'T does from this Lightnings force secure my head.
      Nor will I lift it up so high,
As in the violent Meteors way to lye.
Wealth for its power do we honour and adore?
The things we hate, ill Fate, and Death, have more.

IV

From Towns and Courts, Camps of the Rich
    and Great,
The vast Xerxean Army I retreat,

And to the small Laconick forces fly,
      Which hold the straights of Poverty.
Sellars and Granaries in vain we fill,
      With all the bounteous Summers store,
If the Mind thirst and hunger still.
      The poor rich Man's emphatically poor.
      Slaves to the things we too much prize,
We Masters grow of all that we despise.

V

A Field of Corn, a Fountain and a Wood,
      Is all the Wealth by Nature understood,
The Monarch on whom fertile Nile bestows
      All which that grateful Earth can bear,
      Deceives himself, if he suppose
    That more than this falls to his share.
Whatever an Estate does beyond this afford,
      Is not a rent paid to the Lord;
But is a Tax illegal and unjust,
Exacted from it by the Tyrant Lust.
      Much will always wanting be,
      To him who much desires. Thrice happy He
To whom the wise indulgency of Heaven,
   With sparing hand, but just enough has given.

ODES III, 29

Paraphras'd in Pindarique Verse; and Inscrib'd to the
Right Honourable Lawrence Earl of Rochester

I

Descended of an ancient Line,
   That long the Tuscan Scepter sway'd,
Make haste to meet the generous wine,
   Whose piercing is for thee delay'd:
The rosie wreath is ready made;
   And artful hands prepare
The fragrant Syrian Oyl, that shall perfume thy hair.

II

When the Wine sparkles from a far,
   And the well-natur'd Friend cries, come away;
Make haste, and leave thy business and thy care,
   No mortal int'rest can be worth thy stay.

III

Leave for a while thy costly Country Seat;
   And, to be Great indeed, forget
The nauseous pleasures of the Great:
    Make haste and come:
Come and forsake thy cloying store;
   Thy Turret that surveys, from high,
The smoke, and wealth, and noise of Rome;

And all the busie pageantry
    That wise men scorn, and fools adore:
Come, give thy Soul a loose, and taste the pleasures
    of the poor.

                    IV
Sometimes 'tis grateful to the Rich, to try
A short vicissitude, and fit of Poverty:
        A savoury Dish, a homely Treat,
            Where all is plain, where all is neat,
            Without the stately spacious Room,
The Persian Carpet, or the Tyrian Loom,
Clear up the cloudy foreheads of the Great.

                    V
    The Sun is in the Lion mounted high;
            The Syrian Star
            Barks from a far;
    And with his sultry breath infects the Sky;
The ground below is parch'd, the heav'ns above
    us fry.
        The Shepheard drives his fainting Flock,
            Beneath the covert of a Rock;
        And seeks refreshing Rivulets nigh:
        The Sylvans to their shades retire,
Those very shades and streams, new shades and
    streams require;

And want a cooling breeze of wind to fan the rageing
    fire.

VI

Thou, what befits the new Lord May'r,
And what the City Faction dare,
And what the Gallique Arms will do,
And what the Quiver bearing Foe,
Art anxiously inquisitive to know:
But God has, wisely, hid from humane sight
    The dark decrees of future fate;
    And sown their seeds in depth of night;
He laughs at all the giddy turns of State;
When Mortals search too soon, and fear too late.

VII

Enjoy the present smiling hour;
And put it out of Fortunes pow'r:
The tide of bus'ness, like the running stream,
    Is sometimes high, and sometimes low,
A quiet ebb, or a tempestuous flow,
    And alwayes in extream.
Now with a noiseless gentle course
It keeps within the middle Bed;
Anon it lifts aloft the head,
And bears down all before it, with impetuous force:
    And trunks of Trees come rowling down,

Sheep and their Folds together drown:
Both House and Homested into Seas are borne,
And Rocks are from their old foundations torn,
And woods made thin with winds, their scatter'd
honours mourn.

VIII

Happy the Man, and happy he alone,
He, who can call to day his own:
He, who secure within, can say
To morrow do thy worst, for I have liv'd to day.
Be fair, or foul, or rain, or shine,
The joys I have possest, in spight of fate are mine.
Not Heav'n it self upon the past has pow'r;
But what has been, has been, and I have had my hour.

IX

Fortune, that with malicious joy,
Does Man her slave oppress,
Proud of her Office to destroy,
Is seldome pleas'd to bless:
Still various and unconstant still;
But with an inclination to be ill;
Promotes, degrades, delights in strife,
And makes a Lottery of life.
I can enjoy her while she's kind;
But when she dances in the wind,

And shakes her wings, and will not stay,
        I puff the Prostitute away:
The little or the much she gave, is quietly resign'd:
        Content with poverty, my Soul I arm;
        And Vertue, tho' in rags, will keep me warm.

                    X
            What is 't to me,
Who never sail in her unfaithful Sea,
        If Storms arise, and Clouds grow black?
        If the Mast split and threaten wreck,
Then let the greedy Merchant fear
            For his ill gotten gain;
And pray to Gods that will not hear,
While the debating winds and billows bear
            His Wealth into the Main.
For me secure from Fortunes blows,
(Secure of what I cannot lose,)
In my small Pinnace I can sail,
        Contemning all the blustring roar;
        And running with a merry gale,
    With friendly Stars my safety seek
    Within some little winding Creek;
        And see the storm a shore.

ODES III, 30: *Exegi Monumentum*

'No hands have wrought my monument; no weeds
will hide the nation's footpath to its site.
Tsar Alexander's column it exceeds
   in splendid insubmissive height.

'Not all of me is dust. Within my song,
safe from the worm, my spirit will survive,
and my sublunar frame will dwell as long
   as there is one last bard alive.

'Throughout great Rus' my echoes will extend,
and all will name me, all tongues in her use:
the Slavs' proud heir, the Finn, the Kalmuk, friend
   of steppes, the yet untamed Tunguz.

'And to the people long shall I be dear
because kind feelings did my lyre extoll,
invoking freedom in an age of fear,
   and mercy for the broken soul.'

Obey thy God, and never mind, O Muse,
the laurels or the stings: make it thy rule
to be unstirred by praise as by abuse,
   and do not contradict the fool.

ODES IV, 1

Venus, againe thou mov'st a warre
Long intermitted, pray thee, pray thee spare:
  I am not such, as in the Reigne
Of the good Cynara I was: Refraine,
  Sower Mother of Sweet Loves, forbeare
To bend a man, now at his fiftieth yeare
  Too stubborne for Commands so slack:
Goe where Youths soft intreaties call thee back.
  More timely hie thee to the house,
With thy bright Swans, of Paulus Maximus:
  There jest, and feast, make him thine host,
If a fit livor thou dost seeke to toast;
  For he's both noble, lovely, young,
And for the troubled Clyent fyl's his tongue,
  Child of a hundred Arts, and farre
Will he display the Ensignes of thy warre.
  And when he smiling finds his Grace
With thee 'bove all his Rivals gifts take place,
  He'll thee a Marble Statue make
Beneath a Sweet-wood Roofe, neere Alba Lake:
  There shall thy dainty Nostrill take
In many a Gumme, and for thy soft eares sake
  Shall Verse be set to Harpe and Lute,
And Phrygian Hau'boy, not without the Flute.
  There twice a day in sacred Laies,

The Youths and tender Maids shall sing thy praise:
    And in the Salian manner meet
Thrice 'bout thy Altar with their Ivory feet.
    Me now, nor Wench, nor wanton Boy,
Delights, nor credulous hope of mutuall Joy,
    Nor care I now healths to propound;
Or with fresh flowers to girt my temple round.
    But, why, oh why, my Ligurine,
Flow my thin teares, downe these pale cheeks of mine?
    Or why, my well-grac'd words among,
With an uncomely silence failes my tongue?
    Hard-hearted, I dreame every Night
I hold thee fast! but fled hence, with the Light,
    Whether in Mars his field thou bee,
Or Tybers winding streames, I follow thee.

ODES IV, 7

The snows are fled away, leaves on the shaws
    And grasses in the mead renew their birth,
The river to the river-bed withdraws,
    And altered is the fashion of the earth.

The Nymphs and Graces three put off their fear
    And unapparelled in the woodland play.
The swift hour and the brief prime of the year
    Say to the soul, *Thou wast not born for aye.*

Thaw follows frost; hard on the heel of spring
    Treads summer sure to die, for hard on hers
Comes autumn, with his apples scattering;
    Then back to wintertide, when nothing stirs.

But oh, whate'er the sky-led seasons mar,
  Moon upon moon rebuilds it with her beams;
Come *we* where Tullus and where Ancus are,
  And good Aeneas, we are dust and dreams.

Torquatus, if the gods in heaven shall add
  The morrow to the day, what tongue has told?
Feast then thy heart, for what thy heart has had
  The fingers of no heir will ever hold.

When thou descendest once the shades among,
  The stern assize and equal judgment o'er,
Not thy long lineage nor thy golden tongue,
  No, nor thy righteousness, shall friend thee more.

Night holds Hippolytus the pure of stain,
  Diana steads him nothing, he must stay;
And Theseus leaves Pirithöus in the chain
  The love of comrades cannot take away.

ODES IV, 10

Cruel, and fair! when this soft down,
  (Thy Youths bloom,) shall to bristles grow;
And these fair Curls thy shoulders crown,
  Shall shed, or cover'd be with snow:

When those bright Roses that adorn
  Thy Cheeks shall wither quite away,
And in thy Glass (now made Time's scorn)
  Thou shalt thy changed Face survey.

Then, ah then (sighing) thou'lt deplore
  Thy Ill-spent Youth; and wish, in vain,
Why had I not those thoughts before?
  Or come not my first Looks again?

EPODE II

Happie is he, that from all Businesse cleere,
    As the old race of Mankind were,
With his owne Oxen tills his Sires left lands,
    And is not in the Usurers bands:
Nor Souldier-like started with rough alarmes,
    Nor dreads the Seas inraged harmes:
But flees the Barre and Courts, with the proud bords,
    And waiting Chambers of great Lords.
The Poplar tall, he then doth marrying twine
    With the growne issue of the Vine;
And with his hooke lops off the fruitlesse race,
    And sets more happy in the place:
Or in the bending Vale beholds a-farre
    The lowing herds there grazing are:
Or the prest honey in pure pots doth keepe
    Of Earth, and sheares the tender Sheepe:
Or when that Autumne, through the fields, lifts round
    His head, with mellow Apples crown'd,
How plucking Peares, his owne hand grafted had,
    And purple-matching Grapes, hee's glad!
With which, Priapus, he may thanke thy hands,
    And, Sylvane, thine, that keptst his Lands!
Then now beneath some ancient Oke he may,
    Now in the rooted Grasse him lay,
Whilst from the higher Bankes doe slide the floods;

The soft birds quarrell in the Woods,
The Fountaines murmure as the streames doe creepe,
   And all invite to easie sleepe.
Then when the thundring Jove his Snow and showres
   Are gathering by the Wintry houres;
Or hence, or thence, he drives with many a Hound
   Wild Bores into his toyles pitch'd round:
Or straines on his small forke his subtill nets
   For th' eating Thrush, or Pit-falls sets:
And snares the fearfull Hare, and new-come Crane,
   And 'counts them sweet rewards so ta'en.
Who (amongst these delights) would not forget
   Loves cares so evil, and so great?
But if, to boot with these, a chaste Wife meet
   For houshold aid, and Children sweet;
Such as the Sabines, or a Sun-burnt-blowse,
   Some lustie quick Apulians spouse,
To deck the hallow'd Harth with old wood fir'd
   Against the Husband comes home tir'd;
That penning the glad flock in hurdles by,
   Their swelling udders doth draw dry:
And from the sweet Tub Wine of this yeare takes,
   And unbought viands ready makes:
Not Lucrine Oysters I could then more prize,
   Nor Turbot, nor bright Golden-eyes:
If with bright floods, the Winter troubled much,
   Into our Seas send any such:

Th' Ionian God-wit, nor the Ginny hen
   Could not goe downe my belly then
More sweet then Olives, that new gather'd be
   From fattest branches of the Tree:
Or the herb Sorrell, that loves Meadows still,
   Or Mallowes loosing bodyes ill:
Or at the Feast of Bounds, the Lambe then slaine,
   Or Kid forc't from the Wolfe againe.
Among these Cates how glad the sight doth come
   Of the fed flocks approaching home!
To view the weary Oxen draw, with bare
   And fainting necks, the turned Share!
The wealthy houshold swarme of bondmen met,
   And 'bout the steeming Chimney set!
These thoughts when Usurer Alphius, now about
   To turne mere farmer, had spoke out,
'Gainst th' Ides, his moneys he gets in with paine,
   At th' Calends, puts all out againe.

TIBULLUS

ELEGIES I, 2

With Wine, more Wine, my recent Pains deceive,
Till creeping Slumber send a soft Reprieve:
Asleep, take heed no Whisper stirs the Air,
For wak'd, my Boy, I wake to heart-felt Care.
Now is my Delia watch'd by ruthless Spies,
And the Gate, bolted, all Access denies.
Relentless Gate! may Storms of Wind and Rain,
With mingled Violence avenge my Pain!
May forky Thunders, hurl'd by Jove's red Hand,
Burst every Bolt, and shatter every Band!
Ah no! Rage turns my Brain; the Curse recall;
On me, devoted, let the Thunder fall!
Then recollect my many Wreaths of Yore,
How oft you've seen me weep, insensate Door!
No longer then our Interview delay,
And as you open let no Noise betray.

    In vain I plead! – Dare then my Delia rise!
Love aids the Dauntless, and will blind your Spies!
Those who the Godhead's soft Behests obey,
Steal from their Pillows unobserv'd away;
On tiptoe traverse unobserv'd the Floor;
The Key turn noiseless, and unfold the Door:
In vain the jealous each Precaution take,
Their speaking Fingers Assignations make.

Nor will the God impart to all his Aid:
Love hates the fearful, hates the lazy Maid;
But through sly Windings, and unpractis'd Ways,
His bold Night-Errants to their Wish conveys:
For those whom He with Expectation fires,
No Ambush frightens, and no Labour tires;
Sacred the Dangers of the Dark they dare,
No Robbers stop them, and no Bravoes scare.
Tho' wintery Tempests howl, by Love secure,
The howling Tempest I with ease endure:
No watching hurts me, if my Delia smile,
Soft turn the Gate, and beckon me the while.

   She's mine. Be blind, ye Ramblers of the Night,
Lest angry Venus snatch your guilty Sight:
The Goddess bids her Votaries Joys to be
From every casual Interruption free:
With prying Steps alarm us not, retire,
Nor glare your Torches, nor our Names enquire:
Or if ye know, deny, by Heaven above,
Nor dare divulge the Privacies of Love.
From Blood and Seas vindictive Venus sprung,
And sure Destruction waits the blabbing Tongue!
Nay, should they prate, you, Delia, need not fear;
Your Lord, (a Sorceress swore,) should give no Ear!
By potent Spells she cleaves the sacred Ground,
And shuddering Spectres wildly roam around!

I've seen her tear the Planets from the Sky!
Seen Lightning backward at her Bidding fly!
She calls! from blazing Pyres the Corse descends,
And, re-enliven'd, clasps his wondering Friends!
The Fiends she gathers with a magic Yell,
Then with Aspersions frights them back to Hell!
She wills, – glad Summer gilds the frozen Pole!
She wills, – in Summer wintery Tempests roll!
She knows, ('tis true,) Medea's awful Spell!
She knows to vanquish the fierce Guards of Hell!
To me she gave a Charm for Lovers meet,
('Spit thrice, my Fair, and thrice the Charm repeat.')
Us, in soft Dalliance should your lord surprize;
By this infatuate he'd renounce his Eyes!
But bless no Rival, or th' Affair is known;
This Incantation me befriends alone.
Nor stopp'd she here; but swore, if I'd agree,
By Charms or Herbs to set thy Lover free.
With dire Lustrations she began the Rite!
(Serenely shone the Planet of the Night)
The magic Gods she call'd with hellish sound;
A fable Sacrifice distain'd the Ground —
I stopp'd the Spell: I must not, cannot part:
I begg'd her Aid to gain a mutual Heart.

JAMES GRAINGER

ELEGIES I, 3: *To Messalla*

You'll sail without me through the Aegean sea;
    I hope you and your staff will think of me.
I'm sick and stuck in strange Phaeacia's land:
    Touch me not, greedy Death, with your black hand.
Touch not, dark Death! No mother here with moans
    May gather to her bosom my charred bones,
No sister here may my burnt ash perfume
    With nard or weep dishevelled by my tomb;
Delia's not here, who asked each shrine, they say,
    For oracles, before I went away.

Thrice she drew lots to see what they would tell;
    Thrice said the acolyte that all was well:
All spelled return; unchecked her tears still flowed,
    With many backward glances at my road.
I cheered her, but when all was set to part,
    Wildly sought reasons to delay my start;
Made birds or ominous words pretexts to stay,
    Or claimed I could not leave on Saturn's day.
I set off, but how often did I see
    In each false step presage of misery.
Venture no partings Cupid has not blessed –
    You'll live to know you've flouted his behest!

What is your Isis, Delia, to me now,

Or her brass sistrum rattled to and fro,
Your strict observances, the bathing rites,
    And sleeping chastely all those lonely nights?
Help, goddess, help! Your powers to cure we know,
    And painted tablets in your temples show.
Make Delia, as she promised, veiled in gauze
    Sit out her vigils by your holy doors,
And praise you twice a day with hair unbound,
    Conspicuous, as the Egyptians throng around.
Let me again stand at my household shrine,
    With incense for the Lares of my line.

How well they lived in Saturn's time, before
    Ways were disclosed to every distant shore.
The pine tree had not yet scorned the dark seas,
    Or loosed its bellying canvas to the breeze.
The wandering shipman seeking gain abroad
    Had never heaved his foreign wares on board.
The Bull had not yet bowed his neck beneath
    The yoke, nor steeds champed harness with tame
        teeth.
No dwelling then had doors, no boundary-stone
    Stood on the land to mark out each man's own.
The oaks gave honey; ewes would run to meet
    The carefree farmer, offering him the teat.
No battle-rage was known, nor war's alarms;
    The smith's unfeeling art had not forged arms.

123

But now Jove rules and bloody wounds are rife,
    Drowning, and countless ways of losing life.
O father, spare me; on my heart no lies
    Hang heavy, no false oaths, or blasphemies.
But if I have lived out my fated time,
    Let there be carved above my bones this rhyme:
Here lies Tibullus, snatched by Death's cruel hand,
    Messalla's follower by sea and land.

But since I've never scorned the power Love wields,
    Venus shall lead me to the Elysian fields;
There songs and dances reign, and through the sky
    Birds with sweet voices chirrup as they fly.
The earth untilled bears cassia; all around
    Sweet roses flourish in the generous ground.
There ranks of boys mingling with young girls play;
    There wars begun by love are fought all day.
Those whom Death snatched because of love live there
    Wearing proud wreaths of myrtle in their hair.

The home of evil lies in night profound,
    Obscure, with murky rivers circling round.
With waving snakes for locks Tisiphone
    Storms here and there, while the damned spirits flee.
The black dog Cerberus, with snake-ringed jaws,
    Hisses and watches by the brazen doors.
Bound on his whirling wheel Ixion spins –

124

Juno's assaulter punished for his sins.
Tityos, across nine acres stretched, regales
    The tireless vultures with his black entrails.
Tantalus stands in water, plagued by thirst –
    He bends – but finds the pools have now dispersed.
For slighting Venus' powers Danaus' daughters
    Draw for their leaking vessels Lethe's waters.
This is the place for that man who profanes
    My love, or wishes on me long campaigns.

Delia, be true; some chaperone sit by,
    And zealously protect your chastity;
She can tell stories, and by lamplight pull
    The long thread from the distaff's store of wool;
Tied to their weary tasks the maids sit round,
    And, growing sleepy, drop them to the ground.
Then I'll burst in quite unexpectedly,
    Seeming a god sent to you from the sky.
Then rise, just as you are, with hair untied,
    And run, my Delia, barefoot to my side.

Soon may pale Dawn's pink steeds bring us, I pray,
    The morning star that heralds such a day.

PROPERTIUS

ELEGIES I, 2: *Beauty Unadorned*

Dear girl, what boots it thus to dress thy hair,
Or flaunt in silken garment rich and rare,
To reek of perfume from a foreign mart,
And pass thyself for other than thou art –
Thus Nature's gift of beauty to deface
And rob thy own fair form of half its grace?
Trust me, no skill can greater charms impart:
Love is a naked boy and scorns all art.
Bears not the sod unbidden blossoms rare?
The untrained ivy, is it not most fair?
Greenest the shrub on rocks untended grows,
Brightest the rill in unhewn channel flows.
The beach is with unpolished pebbles gay,
And birds untutored trill the sweetest lay.
Not thus the damsels of the golden age
Were wont the hearts of heroes to engage:

Their loveliness was to no jewels due,
But to such tints as once Apelles drew.
From vain coquettish arts they all were free,
Content to charm with simple modesty.
Less honour from my love I need not fear;
She is well dressed who to one heart is dear.
And thou art numbered with Apollo's choir;
On thee Calliope bestows her lyre,
And then, whose gifts of converse are so sweet?
The gifts of Venus and Minerva meet.
For these by me adored will ever be,
Then bid a long farewell to finery.

ELEGIES I, 20: *Hylas*

Here bubbles out beneath Arganthus' top
A spring, wherein the Thynian nymphs delight.
From boughs uncared for dewy apples drop,
And all around the watered meads are dight
With scarlet poppies and with lilies white.
Boy-like he recked not wherefore he was sent,
But culled with idle hands those garlands bright,
In artless wonder o'er the water bent,
And lingering long admired the charms that mirror
    lent.

Then, stooping from the brink, he stretched his hand
And leaned upon one arm his urn to fill.
At once his beauty charmed the Naiad band,
Who straight unlinked their dance and gazed, until,
Just as the lad hung forward o'er the rill,
They drew him lightly through the yielding tide.
One call for help he gave: then all was still.
Alcides far away in answer cried,
But faint from furthest springs the empty air replied.

ELEGIES II, 1: *To Maecenas*

You ask, why thus my Loves I still rehearse,
Whence the soft strain and ever-melting verse?
From Cynthia all that in my numbers shines;
She is my Genius, she inspires the lines;
No Phoebus else, no other Muse I know,
She tunes my easy rhyme, and gives the lay to flow.
If the loose curls around her forehead play,
Or lawless, o'er their ivory margin stray;
If the thin Coan web her shape reveal,
And half disclose the limbs it should conceal;
Of those loose curls, that ivory front I write;
Of the dear web whole volumes I indite;
Or if to music she the lyre awake,
That the soft subject of my song I make,
And sing with what a careless grace she flings
Her artful hand across the sounding strings.

If sinking into sleep she seem to close
Her languid lids, I favour her repose
With lulling notes, and thousand beauties see
That slumber brings to aid my Poetry.
When, less averse, and yielding to desires,
She half accepts, and half rejects, my fires,
While to retain the envious lawn she tries,
And struggles to elude my longing eyes,
The fruitful Muse from that auspicious night
Dates the long Iliad of the amorous fight.
In brief whate'er she do, or say, or look,
'Tis ample matter for a lover's book;
And many a copious narrative you'll see
Big with the important Nothing's history.

THOMAS GRAY   133

ELEGIES II, 28

When thou must home to shades of under ground,
And there ariv'd, a newe admired guest,
The beauteous spirits do ingirt thee round,
White Iope, blith Hellen, and the rest,
To heare the stories of thy finisht love
From that smoothe toong whose musicke hell
     can move;

Then wilt thou speake of banqueting delights,
Of masks and revels which sweete youth did make,
Of Turnies and great challenges of knights,
And all these triumphes for thy beauties sake:
When thou hast told these honours done to thee,
Then tell, O tell, how thou didst murther me.

ELEGIES II, 29A: *Arrested by Amorini*

Yesterday night, my light, when I was roving drunk
    And had no servants to lead me along,
A crowd of little boys met me (I do not know
    How many – fear stopped me counting them).
I saw that some were carrying little torches, others
    Arrows, and a few had cords to tie me up.
But they were naked. Said a naughtier one of them
    'Arrest this man. You know him well by now.
This was the one the angry woman hired us for.'
    And as he spoke a noose was round my neck.
Then one said 'Push him into the middle', and another
    'He thinks we're not Gods. He must die!
She's been expecting you for hours on end, but you,
    Ungrateful lout, seek someone else's door.
When she's untied the Sidon snood she wears at night
    And opened wide her drowsy eyes,
Fragrance will waft around you, not of Arabian grass
    But made by the hands of Love himself.
Now free him, brothers. Now he promises true love,
    And look, we've now come to the house as ordered'
And with this, putting on my cloak again, they said
      to me
    'Go now and learn to stay at home of nights.'

ELEGIES II, 29B: *An early morning visit*

It was early morning. I wanted to see if she slept alone.
   Yes, Cynthia was alone in bed.
I stood entranced – had never seen her more beautiful,
   Not even when in crimson tunic
She was going off to tell her dreams to chaste Vesta
   For fear of harm to herself or me:
She looked like that, I thought, freshly released
     from sleep.
   Ah, how powerful sheer beauty is!
'What's this?', she said, 'The dawn patrol on mistresses?
   Do you think my morals are like yours?
I'm not so fickle. One tried man's enough for me.
   You perhaps – or someone truer.
You'll find no marks or indentations in the bed,
   No signs that two have tumbled here.
Look, there's no bodily exhalation,
   Not one breath of adulterous guilt.'
She spoke and fending off my kiss with her right hand
   Leapt into bedroom slippers and away.
So I, the would-be guardian of true love, was foiled.
   Since then I've never had a happy night.

ELEGIES IV, 7: *Cynthia's Ghost*

A ghost is something. Death does *not* close all.
  A pale shade escapes, defeating the pyre.
For I have seen Cynthia leaning over my bed-head
  (Though lately buried by the busy road)
While sleep for me was hung up on love's funeral
  And I mourned my bed's cold kingdom.
She had the same hair as when borne to burial,
  The same eyes; but the dress she wore was charred
And the fire had eaten into that beryl on her finger
  And Lethe water had chafed her lips.
Anger and voice were those of the breathing woman
  As her brittle hands snapped their thumbs:

'Traitor, from whom no woman need expect good faith,
  Can you have fallen asleep so soon?
So soon forgotten stolen joys in the wakeful Subura?
  Those tricky nights and my worn windowsill
From which, time and again, I hung on a rope for you,
  Descending hand under hand to your embrace?
We often shared Venus at the crossroads breast to breast,
  Our cloaks warming the road,
Alas for that secret understanding whose specious words
  Deaf southern winds have blown away!

Yes, no.one keened for me as my eyes closed. Had *you*

137

Called me back I'd have gained an extra day.
No watchman rattled a split cane near me
    And the crock against my head hurt.
Besides, who saw you bowed in grief above my body
    Or in a black toga hot with tears?
If it bored you to go further you could at least have
        slowed
    The bearers' pace to the city gates.
Ingrate, why weren't you there to pray for wind for
        the pyre?
    Why were my flames not perfumed with nard?
Was it even too much trouble to strew cheap hyacinths
    And hallow my ashes from a broken wine-jar?

Put Lygdamus to torture! Hot irons for the home-bred
        slave!
    I knew, when I drank the poisoned wine that turned
        me pale.
Though artful Nomas hides away her secret juices
    The fiery potsherd will show whose hands are
        guilty.
Yesterday's prostitute parading for cheap nights
    Now sweeps by in a gold-embroidered gown,
But hands out heavier stints in unfair basket-loads
    To any girl who gabs about my beauty.
For taking garlands to my tomb old Petale
    Must suffer chaining to a filthy clog,

And Lalage is hung up by the hair and flogged
    For daring to ask favours in my name.
You sit by while Madame melts down my golden bust
    To gain a dowry from my cremation.

But I'll not nag, Propertius, much as you deserve it;
    In your books my reign was long.
I swear by the Fates' irrevocable chant
    (So may theTriple Dog not snarl at me)
I have kept faith. If I speak false may vipers
    Hiss in my grave and curl up on my bones.

For beyond the sullen flood two places are assigned
    And the whole crowd rows across on different
        courses.
One carries Clytemnestra's foulness and the Cretan
    Queen's who faked a monstrous wooden cow.
But see, the other group swept along in a flower-
        crowned boat
    To where blest airs caress Elysian roses,
Where numerous lutes and where Cybebe's brazen
        cymbals
    And Lydian plectra twang for turbaned dancers.
Andromeda and Hypermnestra, guileless wives,
    Tell of the well-known perils of their story.
The first complains her arms were bruised by her
        mother's chains

And her hands did not deserve cold rocks.
Hypermnestra tells how her sisters dared an outrage
    And how her own heart quailed at it.
So with death's tears we strive to heal life's loves,
    Though *I* hide all your criminal bad faith.

But now, if you have feelings and are not fast bound
    By Chloris' potions, here are my requests.
See that my nurse Parthenia in frail old age lacks
      nothing;
    Towards you she could have been but was not
      greedy.
Don't let my darling Latris, named for usefulness,
    Hold out the mirror for a new mistress.
And all those verses you have made on my account,
    Please burn them. Cease your boasting about me.
Plant ivy on my grave and let abundant clusters
    Gently bind my bones with tangled tendrils
Where fruitful Anio descends on branchy fields
    And ivory, thanks to Hercules, never yellows.
Here on a column write me a fit epitaph but brief
    So travellers in haste from Rome may read it:

HERE IN TIBURTINE GROUND LIES GOLDEN CYNTHIA,
    BRINGING
    GLORY TO YOUR BANKS, FATHER ANIO.

And pay good heed to dreams that come from the
    Gates of Duty;
  When dreams of duty come they carry weight.
At night we roam around. Night frees imprisoned
    shades
  And Cerberus too can range unchained.
At first light law demands return to Lethe Lake;
  We embark and Charon counts his freight.
Others may own you now. Soon I alone shall hold you.
    You'll be with me and bone on mingled bone
      I'll grind.'

Having thus dealt with me in bitter accusation
  The shade from my embrace faded away.

ELEGIES IV, 11: *Cornelia's Defence*

Weep no more, Paullus, where thy wife is laid:
    At the dark gate thy prayer will beat in vain;
Once let the nether realm receive the shade,
    The adamantine bar turns not again.

Prayer may move Heaven, but, the sad river passed,
    The grave relentless gives not back its dead:
Such sentence spake the funeral trumpet's blast,
    As sank in funeral flames thy loved one's head.

No honours that on Paullus' consort wait,
    No pride of ancestry or storied bust,
Could save Cornelia from her cruel fate:
    Now one small hand may hold her grandeur's dust.

Shades of the Dead and sluggish fens that gloom
  Around Hell's murky shores my steps to bind,
Before my hour, but pure in soul, I come,
  Then let the Judge of all the Dead be kind.

Call the dread Court; let silence reign in Hell;
  Set for an hour the damned from torture free,
And still the Guardian Hound. If aught I tell
  But truth, fall Hell's worst penalty on me.

Is honour to a glorious lineage due?
  What my sires were, Afric and Spain proclaim.
Nor poor the blood I from my mother drew,
  For well may Libo's match with Scipio's name.

And when, my virgin vesture laid aside,
  They set the matron's wreath upon my head,
Thine, Paullus, I became, till death thy bride:
  'Wedded to one' shall on my tomb be read.

By Glory's shrine I swear, great Scipio's tomb,
  Where crownless Afric sits a captive maid,
By him that led the Macedonian home
  In chains and all his pride in ruin laid,

Never for me was bent the censor's law;
    Never by me wrong to your honour done;
Your scutcheon to Cornelia owes no flaw,
    To her your roll of worthy names owes one.

Nor failed my virtue; faithful still I stood,
    And stainless from the bridal to the bier.
No law I needed save my noble blood;
    The basely born are innocent through fear.

Judge strictly as ye will, within the bound
    Of Death's wide realm not one, matron or maid,
Howe'er renowned in story, will be found
    To shun communion with Cornelia's shade.

Not she, the maid of purity unstained,
    At touch of whose chaste hand Cybele moved,
When other hands in vain the cable strained;
    Not she, the virgin of the gods beloved,

For whom, when Vesta's sacred fire was lost,
    It from her votary's robe rekindled sprang.
And thou, dear mother, did thy child e'er cost
    Thee, save by her untimely fate, a pang?

Short was my span, yet children three I bore,
    And in their arms I drew my latest breath;
In these I live although my life is o'er;
    Their dear embraces took the sting from death.

Twice did my brother fill the curule chair,
    There sat he when I parted. Daughter, thou
Wast born a censor's child; be it thy care
    Like me, by wedded troth, his rule to show.

Husband, to thee our pledges I consign,
    Still in my dust there lives a mother's heart;
Around one neck henceforth their arms must twine;
    Father and mother too henceforth thou art.

Kiss for thyself and then for her that's gone;
    Thy loving breast the whole dear burden bears;
Oft as for me thou weepest, weep alone,
    And ere thy children kiss thee dry thy tears.

Be it enough by night thy grief to pour,
    By night to commune with Cornelia's shade;
If to my likeness in thy secret bower
    Thou speakest, speak as though I answer made.

Should time bring on another wedding-day,
    And set a stepdame in your mother's place,
My children, let no looks your gloom betray;
    Kind ways and loving words will win her grace.

Nor speak too much of me; the jealous ear
    Of the new wife perchance offence may take.
But ah! if my poor ashes are so dear
    That he will live unwedded for my sake,

Learn, children, to forestall your sire's decline,
    And let no lonesome thought come near his life;
Add to your years what Fate has reft from mine;
    Blest in my children let him bless his wife.

Though brief my day, I have not lived in vain;
    Mourning for child of mine I never wore;
When from my home went forth my funeral train
    Not one was missing there of all I bore.

My cause is pleaded. Now, ye mourners, rise
    And witness bear till earth my meed decree;
If worth may claim its guerdon in the skies,
    My glorious ancestors may welcome me.

OVID

AMORES I, 13:
Unwelcome Dawn

Too soon Aurora brings the day,
   Too soon she leaves the bed
Beneath the ocean where her lord
   Still rests his ancient head.

Why make such haste, O golden queen,
   Thy chariot to uprear?
This is the hour when most I love
   To feel my darling near.

In the cool breeze the little birds
   Begin their morning song.
But our sound sleep is scarce disturbed
   By the harmonious throng.

Nor men nor maids desire thee yet;
   Thy dew-wet steeds restrain.
Wait for a while, and in thy car
   Hold back the glistening rein.

AMORES II, 8:
To Corinna's Chamber-Maid

Dear skilful Betty, who dost far excel
My Lady's other maids in dressing well:
Dear Betty, fit to be prefer'd above
To Juno's chamber, or the Queen of Love;
Gentle, well-bred, not rustically coy,
Not easy to deny desired joy,
Through whose soft eyes still secret wishes shine,
Fit for thy mistress' use, but more for mine.
Who, Betty, did the fatal secret see,
Who told Corinna you were kind to me?
Yet when she chid me for my kind embrace,
Did any guilty blush spread o'er my face?
Did I betray thee, maid, or could she spy
The least confession in my conscious eye?
Not that I think it a disgrace to prove
Stol'n sweets, or make a chamber-maid my Love.
Achilles wanton'd in Briseis' arms,
Atrides bow'd to fair Cassandra's charms.
Sure I am less than these, then what can bring
Disgrace to me, that so became a king?
But when she lookt on you, poor harmless maid,
You blusht, and all the kind intrigue betray'd:
Yet still I vow'd, I made a stout defence,
I swore and lookt as bold as Innocence:

Damme, egad, all that, and let me die;
Kind Venus, do not hear my perjury,
Kind Venus, stop thy ears when lovers lie.
Now, Betty, how will you my oaths requite?
Come, prithee let's compound for more delight,
Faith, I am easy, and but ask a night.
What! Start at the proposal? how! deny?
Pretend fond fears of a discovery?
Refuse, lest some sad chance the thing betray?
Is this your kind, your damn'd obliging way?
Well, deny on, I'll lie, I'll swear, no more,
Corinna now shall know thou art a whore;
I'll tell, since you my fair address forbid,
How often, when, and where and what we did.

THOMAS CREECH   151

AMORES II, 9: *To Love*

O Love! how cold and slow to take my part
Thou idle wanderer about my heart.
Why thy old faithful soldier wilt thou see
Opprest in thy own tents? They murther me.
Thy flames consume, thy arrows pierce thy friends.
Rather on foes pursue more noble ends.
Achilles' sword would certainly bestow
A cure, as certain as it gave the blow.
Hunters, who follow flying game, give o'er
When the prey's caught; hopes still lead on before.
We, thine own slaves, feel thy tyrannic blows,
Whilst thy tame hand's unmov'd against thy foes.
On men disarm'd how can you gallant prove?
And I was long ago disarm'd by Love.
Millions of dull men live and scornful maids:
We'll own Love valiant when he these invades.

Rome from each corner of the wide world snatch'd
A laurel, or 't had been to this day thatch'd.
But the old soldier has his resting place,
And the good batter'd horse is turn'd to grass:
The harrast whore, who liv'd a wretch to please,
Has leave to be a bawd, and take her ease.
For me then, who have truly spent my blood,
Love, in thy service, and so boldly stood
In Celia's trenches, were 't not wisely done
E'en to retire, and live at peace at home?
No – might I gain a godhead to disclaim
My glorious title to my endless flame,
Divinity with scorn I would forswear,
Such sweet, dear, tempting devils women are!
Whene'er those flames grow faint, I quickly find
A fierce, black storm pour down upon my mind;
Headlong I'm hurl'd, like horsemen who in vain
Their fury-flaming coursers would restrain.
As ships, just when the harbour they attain,
Are snatch'd by sudden blasts to sea again;
So love's fantastic storms reduce my heart
Half rescu'd; and the God resumes his dart.
Strike here, this undefended bosom wound,
And for so brave a conquest be renown'd.
Shafts fly so fast to me from every part,
You'll scarce discern the quiver from my heart.
What wretch can bear a live-long night's dull rest,

Or think himself in lazy slumbers blest?
Fool, is not Sleep the image of pale Death?
There's time for rest, when Fate has stopp'd
      your breath.
Me may my soft deluding dear deceive!
I'm happy in my hopes while I believe;
Now let her flatter, then as fondly chide,
Often may I enjoy, oft be denied!
With doubtful steps the God of war does move,
By thy example of ambiguous love.
Blown to and fro like down from thy own wing,
Who knows when joy or anguish thou wilt bring?
Yet, at thy mother's and thy slave's request,
Fix an eternal empire in my breast;
      And let th' inconstant, charming sex,
      Whose wilful scorn does lovers vex,
      Submit their hearts before thy throne;
      The vassal world is then thy own.

ELEGIES I, 5

In summers heate and mid-time of the day
To rest my limbes upon a bed I lay,
One window shut, the other open stood,
Which gave such light as twincles in a wood,
Like twilight glimps at setting of the Sunne
Or night being past, and yet not day begunne.
Such light to shamefast maidens must be showne,
Where they may sport, and seeme to bee unknowne.
Then came Corinna in a long loose gowne,
Her white neck hid with tresses hanging downe:
Resembling fayre Semiramis going to bed
Or Layis of a thousand wooers sped.
I snacht her gowne, being thin, the harme was small,
Yet striv'd she to be covered there withall.
And striving thus as one that would be cast,
Betray'd her selfe, and yelded at the last.
Starke naked as she stood before mine eye,
Not one wen in her body could I spie.
What armes and shoulders did I touch and see,
How apt her breasts were to be prest by me?
How smooth a belly under her wast saw I?
How large a legge, and what a lustie thigh?
To leave the rest, all lik'd me passing well,
I cling'd her naked body, downe she fell,
Judge you the rest: being tirde she bad me kisse,
Jove send me more such after-noones as this.

CHRISTOPHER MARLOWE   155

From ELEGIES I, 8: *The Bawd*

There is a Bawd renown'd in Venus Wars,
And dreadfull still with honourable scars:
Her youth and beauty, craft and guile supply
Sworn Foe to all degrees of Chastity.
Dypsas who first taught Love sick Maids the way
To cheat the Bridegroom on the Wedding day.
And then a hundred subtile tricks devis'd,
Wherewith the Amorous Theft might be disguis'd.
Of Pigeons-blood, squeez'd from the panting heart,
With Surfeit-water to contract the part,
She knows the Use: whilst the good man betray'd,
With eager Arms huggs the false bleeding Maid.
Of herbs and Spells she tries the Guilty Force,
The poyson of a Mare that goes to Horse.
Cleaving the Midnight Air upon a Switch,
Some for a Bawd, most take her for a Witch.
Each Morning sees her reeling to her Bed,
Her Native Blew o'ercome with drunken red.
Her ready Tongue ne'er wants an usefull lie,
Soft moving words, nor Charming flattery.

ELEGIES I, 14

Leave colouring thy tresses I did cry,
Now hast thou left no haires at all to die.
But what had beene more faire had they beene kept?
Beyond thy robes thy dangling lockes had sweept.
Feardst thou to dresse them being fine and thinne
Like to the silke the curious Seres spinne,
Or thrids which spiders slender foote drawes out
Fastning her light web some old beame about?
Not black, nor golden were they to our viewe,
Yet although neither mixt of eithers hue,
Such as in hilly Idas watry plaines,
The Cedar tall spoyld of his barke retaines.
And they were apt to curle an hundred waies,
And did to thee no cause of dolour raise.
Nor hath the needle, or the combes teeth reft them,
The maide that kembd them ever safely left them.

Oft was she drest before mine eyes, yet never,
Snatching the combe, to beate the wench out drive her.
Oft in the morne her haires not yet digested,
Halfe sleeping on a purple bed she rested,
Yet seemely like a Thracian Bacchinall
That tyr'd doth rashly on the greene grasse fall.
When they were slender, and like downy mosse,
Thy troubled haires, alas, endur'd great losse.
How patiently hot irons they did take
In crooked trannells crispy curles to make.
I cryed, tis sinne, tis sinne, these haires to burne,
They well become thee, then to spare them turne.
Farre off be force, no fire to them may reach,
Thy very haires will the hot bodkin teach.
Lost are the goodly lockes, which from their crowne
Phœbus and Bacchus wisht were hanging downe.
Such were they as Diana painted stands
All naked holding in her wave-moist hands.
Why doest thy ill kembd tresses losse lament?
Why in thy glasse doest looke being discontent?
Bee not to see with wonted eyes inclinde,
To please thy selfe, thy selfe put out of minde.
No charmed herbes of any harlot skathd thee,
No faithlesse witch in Thessale waters bath'd thee.
No sicknesse harm'd thee, farre be that away,
No envious tongue wrought thy thicke lockes decay.
By thine owne hand and fault thy hurt doth growe,

158

Thou mad'st thy head with compound poyson flow.
Now Germany shall captive haire-tyers send thee,
And vanquisht people curious dressings lend thee,
Which some admiring, O thou oft wilt blush
And say he likes me for my borrowed bush,
Praysing for me some unknowne Guelder dame,
But I remember when it was my fame.
Alas she almost weepes, and her white cheekes,
Died red with shame, to hide from shame she seekes.
She holds, and viewes her old lockes in her lappe,
Aye me, rare gifts unworthy such a happe.
Cheere up thy selfe, thy losse thou maiest repaire,
And be heerafter seene with native haire.

From METAMORPHOSES I:
The Flight of Daphne

As when a hare the speedy greyhound spies,
His feet for prey, she hers for safety plies –
Now bears he up; now, now he hopes to fetch her,
And with his snout extended strains to catch her:
Not knowing whether caught or no, she slips
Out of his wide-stretch'd jaws and touching lips. –
The god and virgin in such strife appear,
He quicken'd by his hope, she by her fear;
But the pursuer doth more nimble prove,
Enabled by th' industrious wings of love.
Nor gives he time to breathe: now at her heels,
His breath upon her dangling hair she feels.
Clean-spent and fainting, her affrighted blood
Forsakes her cheeks. She cries unto the Flood.
'Help, Father, if your streams contain a Power –

160

May Earth, for too well pleasing, me devour!
Or, by transforming, O destroy this shape,
That thus betrays me to undoing rape.'
Forthwith a numbness all her limbs possesst,
And slender films her softer sides invest.
Hair into leaves, her arms to branches grow,
And late swift feet, now roots, are less than slow.
Her graceful head a leafy top sustains,
One beauty throughout all her form remains.
Still Phoebus loves: he handles the new plant,
And feels her heart within the bark to pant,
Embrac'd the bole, as he would her have done,
And kiss'd the boughs: the boughs his kisses shun.

From METAMORPHOSIS II:
The Palace of the Sun

Sublime on lofty columns, bright with gold
And fiery carbuncle, its roof inlaid
With ivory, rose the Palace of the Sun,
Approached by folding gates with silver sheen
Radiant; material priceless, – yet less prized
For its own worth than what the cunning hand
Of Mulciber thereon had wrought, – the globe
Of Earth, – the Seas that wash it round, – the Skies
That overhang it. 'Mid the waters played
Their Gods caerulean. Triton with his horn
Was there, and Proteus of the shifting shape,
And old Aegeon, curbing with firm hand
The monsters of the deep. Her Nereids there
Round Doris sported, seeming, some to swim,
Some on the rocks their tresses green to dry,

Some dolphin-borne to ride; nor all in face
The same, nor different; – so should sisters be.
Earth showed her men, and towns, and woods,
        and beasts,
And streams, and Nymphs, and rural Deities:
And over all the mimic Heaven was bright
With the twelve Zodiac signs, on either valve
Of the great portal figured, – six on each.

    And now the child of Clymene, the steep
Ascending, passed the threshold of his Sire,
Yet unassured, and towards the Godhead bent
His steps, yet far off stood, nor nearer bore
The dazzling radiance. Clad in flowing robe
Of purple, on a throne of state, that shone
Crusted with beryl, Phoebus sate. To right
And left were ranged the Days, and Months,
        and Years,
And Ages, and the Hours, with each its space
Allotted equal. Spring, with flowery crown
Round his young brows, – and Summer, lightly clad,
With wreath of odorous spices, – Autumn, stained
With juice of trodden wine-press, – and the head
Of Winter, white with frost and age, – were there.
Himself sits midmost: – nor escapes his eye
All-seeing long the youth, with wondering awe
Such marvels viewing: – and 'What brings thee here,
My offspring, – for I recognise thee such, –

What wouldst thou of me?' asks the God. To whom
The youth – 'O common light of all the world,
Phoebus, my Sire, if by such name I dare
Address thee, nor hath Clymene her shame
With falsehood sought to veil, – give me, I pray,
Some pledge whereby henceforth I may be known
Thy son indeed, and all this doubt be cleared!'
He said – and straight the Godhead laid aside
The dazzling glories of his brow, and bade
Approach, and folded in his arms his child,
And – 'O well worthy to be owned my Son,'
He said, 'Thy Mother's tale was truth. To still
All question, ask what boon thou wilt – ere asked
I grant it thee. By Styx, dread oath of Gods,
Which never yet these rays illumed, I swear!'

From METAMORPHOSIS III:

Echo and Narcissus

The hearts of dyvers trim yong men his beautie
>   gan to move
And many a Ladie fresh and faire was taken in his love.
But in that grace of Natures gift such passing pride
>   did raigne,
That to be toucht of man or Mayde he wholy did disdaine.
A babling Nymph that Echo hight, who hearing
>   others talke,
By no meanes can restraine hir tongue but that it
>   needes must walke,
Nor of hir selfe hath powre to ginne to speake to any
>   wight,
Espyde him dryving into toyles the fearefull stagges
>   of flight.
This Echo was a body then and not an onely voyce.
Yet of hir speach she had that time no more than now
>   the choyce,
That is to say, of many wordes the latter to repeate.
The cause thereof was Junos wrath. For when that
>   with the feate
She might have often taken Jove in daliance with
>   his Dames,
And that by stealth and unbewares in middes of all
>   his games,

This elfe would with hir tatling talke deteine hir
    by the way,
Untill that Jove had wrought his will and they were
    fled away.
The which when Juno did perceyve, she said with
    wrathfull mood:
This tongue that hath deluded me shall doe thee little
    good,
For of thy speach but simple use hereafter shalt thou have.
The deede it selfe did straight confirme the
    threatnings that she gave.
Yet Echo of the former talke doth double oft the ende
And backe againe with just report the wordes earst
    spoken sende.
  Now when she sawe Narcissus stray about the
    Forrest wyde,
  She waxed warme and step for step fast after him
    she hyde.
The more she followed after him and neerer that
    she came,
The hoter ever did she waxe as neerer to hir flame.
Lyke as the lively Brimstone doth which dipt about
    a match,
And put but softly to the fire, the flame doth lightly
    catch.
O Lord how often woulde she faine (if nature would
    have let)

Entreated him with gentle wordes some favour for
    to get?
But nature would not suffer hir nor give hir leave
    to ginne.
Yet (so farre forth as she by graunt at natures hande
    could winne)
As readie with attentive eare she harkens for some
    sounde,
Whereto she might replie hir wordes, from which she
    is not bounde.
By chaunce the stripling being strayde from all his
    companie,
Sayde: Is there any body nie? Straight Echo answerde: I.
Amazde he castes his eye aside, and looketh round
    about,
And Come (that all the Forrest roong) aloud he calleth
    out.
And Come (sayth she:) he looketh backe, and seeing no
    man followe,
Why fliste, he cryeth once againe: and she the same
    doth hallowe.
He still persistes and wondring much what kinde of
    thing it was
From which that answering voyce by turne so duely
    seemde to passe,
Said: Let us joyne. She (by hir will desirous to have said
In fayth with none more willingly at any time or stead)

Said: Let us joyne. And standing somewhat in hir owne
    conceit,
Upon these wordes she left the Wood, and forth she
    yeedeth streit,
To coll the lovely necke for which she longed had so
    much,
He runnes his way and will not be imbraced of no such,
And sayth: I first will die ere thou shalt take of me thy
    pleasure.
She aunswerde nothing else thereto, but Take of me
    thy pleasure.
Now when she saw hir selfe thus mockt, she gate hir to
    the Woods,
And hid hir head for verie shame among the leaves
    and buddes.
And ever sence she lyves alone in dennes and hollow
    Caves,
Yet stacke hir love still to hir heart, through which she
    dayly raves
The more for sorrowe of repulse. Through restlesse
    carke and care
Hir bodie pynes to skinne and bone, and waxeth
    wonderous bare.
The bloud doth vanish into ayre from out of all hir
    veynes,
And nought is left but voyce and bones: the voyce yet
    still remaynes:

Hir bones they say were turnde to stones. From thence
    she lurking still
In Woods, will never shewe hir head in field nor yet on
    hill.

Narcissus falls in Love with Himself
The stripling wearie with the heate and hunting in
    the chace,
And much delighted with the spring and coolenesse of
    the place,
Did lay him downe upon the brim: and as he stooped
    lowe
To staunche his thurst, another thurst of worse effect
    did growe.
For as he dranke, he chaunst to spie the Image of
    his face,
The which he did immediately with fervent love
    embrace.
He feedes a hope without cause why. For like a foolishe
    noddie
He thinkes the shadow that he sees, to be a lively boddie.
Astraughted like an ymage made of Marble stone he lyes,
There gazing on his shadowe still with fixed staring eyes.
Stretcht all along upon the ground, it doth him good
    to see
His ardant eyes which like two starres full bright and
    shyning bee,

And eke his fingars, fingars such as Bacchus might
    beseeme,
And haire that one might worthely Apollos haire it
    deeme,
His beardlesse chinne and yvorie necke, and eke the
    perfect grace
Of white and red indifferently bepainted in his face.
All these he woondreth to beholde, for which (as I doe
    gather)
Himselfe was to be woondred at, or to be pitied rather.
He is enamored of himselfe for want of taking heede,
And where he lykes another thing, he lykes himselfe
    in deede.
He is the partie whome he wooes, and suter that doth
    wooe,
He is the flame that settes on fire, and thing that
    burneth tooe.
O Lord how often did he kisse that false deceitfull
    thing?
How often did he thrust his armes midway into the
    spring
To have embraste the necke he saw and could not catch
    himselfe?
He knowes not what it was he sawe. And yet the foolish
    elfe
Doth burne in ardent love thereof. The verie selfsame
    thing

170

That doth bewitch and blinde his eyes, encreaseth all
his sting.

The Lament of Narcissus
It is my selfe I well perceyve, it is mine Image sure,
That in this sort deluding me, this furie doth procure.
I am inamored of my selfe, I doe both set on fire,
And am the same that swelteth too, through impotent
desire.
What shall I doe? be woode or woo? whome shall I
woo therefore?
The thing I seeke is in my selfe, my plentie makes me
poore.
I would to God I for a while might from my bodie part.
This wish is straunge to heare, a Lover wrapped all in
smart
To wish away the thing the which he loveth as his heart.
My sorrowe takes away my strength. I have not long
to live,
But in the floure of youth must die. To die it doth not
grieve.
For that by death shall come the ende of all my griefe
and paine
I would this yongling whome I love might lenger life
obtaine:
For in one soule shall now decay we stedfast Lovers
twaine.

171

This saide in rage he turnes againe unto the
    forsaide shade,
And rores the water with the teares and sloubring
    that he made,
That through his troubling of the Well his ymage gan
    to fade . . .
As lith and supple waxe doth melt against the burning
    flame,
Or morning dewe against the Sunne that glareth on
    the same:
Even so by piecemale being spent and wasted through
    desire,
Did he consume and melt away with Cupids secret fire.
His lively hue of white and red, his cheerefulnesse and
    strength
And all the things that lyked him did wanze away at
    length.
So that in fine remayned not the bodie which of late
The wretched Echo loved so. Who when she sawe his
    state,
Although in heart she angrie were, and mindefull of his
    pride,
Yet ruing his unhappie case, as often as he cride
Alas, she cride, Alas likewise with shirle redoubled
    sound.
And when he beate his breast, or strake his feete
    against the ground,

She made like noyse of clapping too. These are the
    woordes that last
Out of his lippes beholding still his woonted ymage past:
Alas sweete boy belovde in vaine, farewell. And by
    and by
With sighing sound the selfesame wordes the Echo
    did reply.
With that he layde his wearie head against the grassie
    place
And death did cloze his gazing eyes that woondred at
    the grace
And beautie which did late adorne their Masters
    heavenly face.
And afterward when into Hell receyved was his spright
He goes me to the Well of Styx, and there both day
    and night
Standes tooting on his shadow still as fondely as before.

From METAMORPHOSIS V:
Proserpine and Dis

Neare Enna walles there standes a Lake: Pergusa is
    the name.
Cayster heareth not mo songs of Swannes than doth
    the same.
A wood environs everie side the water round about,
And with his leaves as with a veyle doth keepe the
    Sunne heate out.
The boughes do yeelde a coole fresh Ayre: the
    moystnesse of the grounde
Yeeldes sundrie flowres: continuall spring is all the
    yeare there founde.
While in this garden Proserpine was taking hir
    pastime,
In gathering eyther Violets blew, or Lillies white
    as Lime,

And while of Maidenly desire she fillde hir Maund
    and Lap,
Endevoring to outgather hir companions there. By hap
Dis spide hir: lovde hir: caught hir up: and all at once
    well neere,
So hastie, hote, and swift a thing is Love, as may
    appeare.
The Ladie with a wailing voyce afright did often call
Hir Mother and hir waiting Maides, but Mother most
    of all.
And as she from the upper part hir garment would
    have rent,
By chaunce she let her lap slip down, and out the
    flowres went.
And such a sillie simplenesse hir childish age yet
    beares,
That even the verie losse of them did move hir more
    to teares.

From METAMORPHOSIS X:
Orpheus and Eurydice

So sang he, and, accordant to his plaint,
As wailed the strings, the bloodless Ghosts were
     moved
To weeping. By the lips of Tantalus
Unheeded slipped the wave; – Ixion's wheel
Forgot to whirl; the Vulture's bloody feast
Was stayed; awhile the Belides forbore
Their leaky urns to dip; and Sisyphus
Sate listening on his stone. Then first, they say,
The iron cheeks of the Eumenides
Were wet with pity. Of the nether realm
Nor King nor Queen had heart to say him nay.
Forth from a host of new-descended Shades
Eurydice was called; and, halting yet,
Slow with her recent wound she came – alive

176

On one condition to her Spouse restored,
That, till Avernus' vale is passed and Earth
Regained, he look not backward, or the boon
Is null and forfeit. Through the silent realm
Upward against the steep and fronting hill
Dark with obscurest gloom, the way he led:
And now the upper air was all but won,
When, fearful lest the toil o'ertask her strength,
And yearning to behold the form he loved,
An instant back he looked, – and back the Shade
That instant fled! The arms that wildly strove
To clasp and stay had clasped but yielding air!
No word of plaint even in that second Death
Against her Lord she uttered, – how could Love
Too anxious be upbraided? – but one last
And sad 'Farewell,' scarce audible, she sighed,
And vanished to the Ghosts that late she left.

From METAMORPHOSIS XI:
Cave of Somnus

Near the Cimmerian Land, deep-caverned, lies
A hollow mount, the home of sluggish Sleep;
Where never ray from morn or evening skies
Can enter, but where blackening vapours creep,
And doubtful gloom unbroken sway doth keep.

There never crested bird evokes the dawn,
Nor watchful dogs disturb the silence deep,
Nor wandering beast, nor forest tempest-torn,
Nor harsher sound of human passions born.

Mute quiet reigns; – but from the lowest cave
A spring Lethaean rising evermore
Pours through the murmuring rocks a slumberous
     wave.
The plenteous poppy blossoms at the door,
And countless herbs, of night the drowsy store.

From METAMORPHOSIS XIII:
Polyphemus Pleads His Suit

'O lovely Galatea, whiter far
Than falling snows, and rising lilies are;
More flowery than the meads, as crystal bright,
Erect as alders, and of equal height:
More wanton than a kid; more sleek thy skin,
Than orient shells that on the shores are seen:
Than apples fairer, when the boughs they lade,
Pleasing as winter suns or summer shade:
More grateful to the sight than goodly planes,
And softer to the touch than down of swans,
Or curds new turn'd; and sweeter to the taste
Than swelling grapes, that to the vintage haste:
More clear than ice, or running streams, that stray
Through garden plots, but ah! more swift than they.
    Yet, Galatea, harder to be broke

Than bullocks, unreclaim'd to bear the yoke,
And far more stubborn than the knotted oak:
Like sliding streams, impossible to hold;
Like them fallacious; like their fountains, cold:
More warping than the willow, to decline
My warm embrace; more brittle than the vine;
Immovable, and fix'd in thy disdain:
Rough, as these rocks, and of a harder grain;
More violent than is the rising flood:
And the prais'd peacock is not half so proud:
Fierce as the fire, and sharp as thistles are,
And more outrageous than a mother bear:
Deaf as the billows to the vows I make,
And more revengeful than a trodden snake:
In swiftness fleeter than the flying hind,
Or driven tempests, or the driving wind.
All other faults with patience I can bear,
But swiftness is the vice I only fear.

   Yet, if you knew me well, you would not shun
My love, but to my wish'd embraces run:
Would languish in your turn, and court my stay;
And much repent of your unwise delay.

From METAMORPHOSIS XV:
On His After-Fame

And now the work is ended, which Jove's rage,
Nor fire, nor sword shall raze, nor eating age.
Come when it will my death's uncertain hour,
Which of this body only hath a power,
Yet shall my better part transcend the sky,
And my immortal name shall never die.
For, wheresoe'er the Roman eagles spread
Their conquering wings, I shall of all be read;
And, if we poets true presages give,
I in my Fame eternally shall live.

GEORGE SANDYS

From TRISTIA III, 3:
To His Wife at Rome, When He was Sick

But thou – for after death I shall be free, –
Fetch home these bones, and what is left of me,
A few flowers give them, with some balm, and lay
Them in some suburb-grave, hard by the way:
And, to inform posterity who's there,
This sad inscription let my marble wear,
'Here lies the soft-soul'd lecturer of love,
Whose envy'd wit did his own ruin prove.
But thou – whoe'er thou beest – that passing by
Lendst to this sudden stone a hasty eye,
If e'er thou knew'st of love the sweet disease,
Grudge not to say, may Ovid rest in peace!'
This for my tomb: but for my books they'll see
More strong and lasting monuments of me,
Which I believe – though fatal – will afford

An endless name unto their ruin'd lord.
And now thus gone, it rests for love of me
Thou shew'st some sorrow to my memory;
Thy funeral offerings to my ashes bear,
With wreaths of cypress bath'd in many a tear.
Though nothing there but dust of me remain,
Yet shall that dust perceive thy pious pain.
But I have done, and my tir'd sickly head,
Though I would fain write more, desires the bed;
Take then this word – perhaps my last to tell –
Which though I want, I wish it thee, farewell!

HENRY VAUGHAN

SENECA

THE QUIET LIFE

Climb at Court for me that will
Tottering favour's pinnacle;
All I seek is to lie still.
Settled in some secret nest
In calm leisure let me rest,
And far off the public stage
Pass away my silent age.
Thus when without noise, unknown,
I have liv'd out all my span,
I shall die, without a groan,
An old honest country man.
Who expos'd to others' eyes,
Into his own heart ne'er pries,
Death to him's a strange surprise.

NOTHINGNESS

After death nothing is, and nothing death;
The utmost limits of a gasp of breath.
Let the ambitious zealot lay aside
His hopes of Heaven (whose faith is but his pride);
Let slavish souls lay by their fear,
Nor be concern'd which way, or where,
After this life they shall be hurl'd:
Dead, we become the lumber of the world,
And to that mass of matter shall be swept,
Where things destroy'd with things unborn are kept;
Devouring Time swallows us whole,
Impartial Death confounds body and soul.
For Hell and the foul fiend that rules
    The everlasting fiery goals,
Devis'd by rogues, dreaded by fools,
With his grim gisly dog that keeps the door,
    Are senseless stories, idle tales,
Dreams, whimsies, and no more.

PETRONIUS
ARBITER

DOING, A FILTHY
PLEASURE IS

Doing, a filthy pleasure is, and short;
And done, we straight repent us of the sport:
Let us not then rush blindly on unto it,
Like lustfull beasts, that onely know to doe it:
For lust will languish, and that heat decay,
But thus, thus, keeping endlesse Holy-day,
Let us together closely lie, and kisse,
There is no labour, nor no shame in this;
This hath pleas'd, doth please, and long will please;
    never
Can this decay, but is beginning ever.

SMALL HOUSE AND
QUIET ROOF TREE

Small house and quiet roof tree, shadowing elm,
Grapes on the vine and cherries ripening,
Red apples in the orchard, Pallas' tree
Breaking with olives, and well-watered earth,
And fields of kale and heavy creeping mallows
And poppies that will surely bring me sleep.
And if I go a-snaring for the birds
Or timid deer, or angling the shy trout,
'Tis all the guile that my poor fields will know.
Go now, yea, go, and sell your life, swift life,
For golden feasts. If the end waits me too,
I pray it find me here, and here shall ask
The reckoning from me of the vanished hours.

LAID ON MY BED IN
SILENCE
OF THE NIGHT

Laid on my bed in silence of the night,
  I scarce had given my weary eyes to sleep,
When Love the cruel caught me by the hair,
  And roused me, bidding me his vigil keep.
'O thou my slave, thou of a thousand loves,
  Canst thou, O hard of heart, lie here alone?'
Bare-foot, ungirt, I raise me up and go,
  I seek all roads, and find my road in none.
I hasten on, I stand still in the way,
Ashamed to turn back, and ashamed to stay.
There is no sound of voices, hushed the streets,
  Not a bird twitters, even the dogs are still.
I, I alone of all men dare not sleep,
  But follow, Lord of Love, thy imperious will.

MARTIAL

EPIGRAMS I, 3

So, they've summed you up, my little book.
You're now 'a milestone in ironic outlook.'
This the price of your publicity:
MARTIAL VIEWS LIFE VERY SAUCILY.
Whatever they say is a load of balls
Certain to send you to second-hand stalls,
Unaware, little book, of the comforts of home
Your 'low key wit' now belongs to Rome.
What today's 'an incandescent event'
Soon winds up 'a minor supplement.'
To set you off on the proper foot
Some shit's written 'Magic, a classic to boot.'

EPIGRAMS I, 4

Caesar, if my small book should reach your hands,
  Relax the frown that dominates all lands.
Jokes are the custom at your triumphs too –
  The general's not ashamed the jokes are blue.
As you watch mimes or dancers on the stage –
  With that expression look upon my page.
These games are harmless, censor: let them pass.
  My poems play around; but not my life.

ALISTAIR ELLIOT

EPIGRAMS V, 9

A slight cold or a touch of flu,
but when THE SPECIALIST and all his crew
of a 100 students once are through,
and every inch of me's been handled twice
by a hundred medics' hands as cold as ice,
the pneumonia I didn't have I DO!

EPIGRAMS IX, 54

If I had hillside olives to fatten fieldfares
    or Sabine woods strung with gins
to cruelly carry hot bodies from the sky
    or could conduct like lightning
small morsels down on a stick, to walk
    grand garnerer of their flutterings,
crop on crop in my meadows of death:
    then I would send you these in token
of love, that you might bite their flesh
    as it were mine. Alas, my fields are asphalt
and listen only to the songs of starlings,
    the fidgeting of finches. The green
of tapered hedges hides the shrill sparrow,
    here the magpie suffers an air-change
to death's bird, while the banished kite
    haunts open fields, the only free man
in a heritage of dependence. Instead,
    I offer you the imagination of birds
whose hard eye drops on the brown earth
    without pardon: come to the start
of the world, we will deal with things cruelly
    as we have love and an inclination to.

EPIGRAMS X, 61

Underneath this greedy stone,
Lies little sweet Erotion;
Whom the fates, with hearts as cold,
Nipt away at six years old.
Thou, whoever thou mayst be,
That hast this small field after me,
Let the yearly rites be paid
To her little slender shade;
So shall no disease or jar
Hurt thy house, or chill thy Lar;
But this tomb here be alone,
The only melancholy stone.

EPIGRAMS II, 53

Would'st thou be free? I fear thou art in jest
But if thou would'st, this is the only law;
Be no man's tavern nor domestic guest:
Drink wholesome wine which thy own servants draw.

Of knavish Carlo scorn the ill-got plate,
The num'rous servants and the cringing throng:
With a few friends on fewer dishes eat,
And let thy clothes, like mine, be plain and strong.

Such friendships make as thou may'st keep with ease;
Great men expect what good men hate to pay;
Be never thou thyself in pain to please,
But leave to fools and knaves th' uncertain prey.

Let thy expense with thy estate keep pace;
Meddle with no man's business, save thine own:
Contented pay for a plebeian face,
And leave vain fops the beauties of the town.

If to this pitch of virtue thou canst bring
Thy mind, thou 'rt freer than the Persian king.

CHARLES SEDLEY   201

EPIGRAMS VI, 11

You wonder now that no man sees
    Such friends as those of ancient Greece.
Here lies the point – Orestes' meat
    Was just the same his friend did eat;
Nor can it yet be found his wine
    Was better, Pylades! than thine.
In home-spun russet I am drest,
    Your cloth is always of the best.
But, honest Marcus, if you please
    To choose me for your Pylades,
Remember, words alone are vain;
    Love – if you would be lov'd again.

EPIGRAMS VI, 12

The golden hair that Galla wears
    Is hers: who would have thought it?
She swears 'tis hers, and true she swears,
    For I know where she bought it.

SIR JOHN HARINGTON

EPIGRAMS X, 23

At length, my friend (while time with still career
Wafts on his gentle wing this eightieth year),
Sees his past days safe out of Fortune's pow'r,
Nor dreads approaching fate's uncertain hour;
Reviews his life, and, in the strict survey,
Finds not one moment he could wish away,
Pleas'd with the series of each happy day.
Such, such a man extends his life's short space,
And from the goal again renews the race:
For he lives twice who can at once employ
The present well, and e'en the past enjoy.

EPIGRAMS X, 47

Things that can bless a life and please,
    Sweetest Martial, they are these:
A store well left, not gain'd with toil,
    A house thine own and pleasant soil,
No strife, small state, a mind at peace,
    Free strength, and limbs free from disease,
Wise innocent friends, like and good,
    Unarted meat, kind neighbourhood,
No Drunken rest, from cares yet free,
    No sadd'ning spouse, yet chaste to thee,
Sleeps, that long Nights abbreviate,
    Because 'tis likening thy wish'd state,
Nor fear'd, nor joy'd at Death or Fate.

EPIGRAMS XI, 104

Prithee die and set me free,
   Or else be
Kind and brisk, and gay like me;
I pretend not to the wise ones,
   To the grave, to the grave,
Or the precise ones.

'Tis not Cheeks, nor Lips nor Eyes,
   That I prize,
Quick Conceits, or sharp Replies,
If wise thou wilt appear, and knowing,
   Repartie, Repartie
To what I'm doing.

Prithee why the Room so dark?
   Not a Spark
Left to light me to the mark;
I love day-light and a candle,
   And to see, and to see,
As well as handle.

Why so many Bolts and Locks,
    Coats and Smocks,
And those Drawers with a Pox?
I could wish, could Nature make it,
    Nakedness, Nakedness
It self were naked.

But if a Mistress I must have,
    Wise and grave,
Let her so her self behave
All the day long Susan Civil,
    Pap by night, pap by night,
Or such a Divel.

EPIGRAMS XI, 104

Prythee die and set me free
   Or else be
Kind and brisk and gay like me.
I pretend not to the wise ones,
   To the grave,
To the grave or the precise ones.

Prythee, why those bolts and locks,
   Coats and smocks?
And those drawers? With a pox!
I would wish, could nature make it,
   Nakedness
Nakedness itself more naked.

Prythee, why the room so dark?
   Not a spark
Left to light me to the mark.
I love daylight or a candle,
   And to see,
And to see as well as handle.

There is neither art nor itch
    In thy breech;
Nor provoking hand or speech.
And when I expect thy motion,
    Fall'st asleep,
Fall'st asleep, or to devotion.

But if a mistress I must have
    Wise and grave,
Let her so herself behave:
By daylight a Susan Civil,
    Nell by night,
Nell by night, or such a devil.

EPIGRAMS XI, 104

Sweet spouse, you must presently troop and be gone,
    Or fairly submit to your betters;
Unless for the faults that are past you atone,
    I must knock off my conjugal fetters.

When at night I am paying the tribute of love –
    You know well enough what's my meaning –
You scorn to assist my devotions, or move,
    As if all the while you were dreaming.

At cribbage and put and all-fours I have seen
    A porter more passion expressing
Than thou, wicked Kate, in the rapturous scene,
    And the height of the amorous blessing.

Then say I to myself, 'Is my wife made of stone,
    Or does the old serpent possess her?'
Better motion and vigour by far might be shown
    By dull sponge of a German professor.

So, Kate, take advice and reform in good time,
    And while I'm performing my duty,
Come in for your club, and repent of desire
    Of paying all scores with your beauty.

But when you're in bed with your master and king,
    That tales out of school ne'er does trumpet,
Move, wriggle, heave, pant, dip round like a ring:
    In short, be as lewd as a strumpet.

EPIGRAMS XII, 46

In all thy humours, whether grave or mellow,
Thou'rt such a touchy, testy, pleasant fellow;
Hast so much wit, and mirth, and spleen about thee,
There is no living with thee, or without thee.

JOSEPH ADDISON

EPIGRAMS XII, 50

None equal you in trees for ever green:
Your bath's the most majestic can be seen:
Your colonnade is lofty, spacious, fine:
And under-foot your marble pavements shine:
Round your wide park the fleeting courser bounds:
Many cascades salute us with their sounds:
Apartments grand: no place to eat or sleep!
What a most noble house you do not keep.

WILLIAM HAY

EPIGRAMS IV, 13

Strange Claudia's married to a friend of mine,
O Hymen, be thou ready with thy pine!
Thus the rare cinnamons with the spikenard join,
And the Thesean sweets with Massic wine.
Nor better do the elm and vine embrace,
Nor the lote trees affect the fenny place,
   Nor yet the myrtles more
   Love and desire the shore.
Let a perpetual peace surround their bed,
And may their loves with equal fire be fed!
May she so love him old, that to him she,
Though old indeed, may not seem so to be.

EPIGRAMS X, 23

Now Antoninus, in a smiling age,
Counts of his life the fifteenth finished stage.
The rounded days and the safe years he sees,
Nor fears death's water mounting round his knees.

To him remembering not one day is sad,
Not one but that its memory makes him glad.
So good men lengthen life; and to recall
The past is to have twice enjoyed it all.

ROBERT LOUIS STEVENSON

EPIGRAMS XI, 27

Milo's from home; and, Milo being gone,
His lands bore nothing, but his wife a son:
Why she so fruitful, and so bare the field?
The lands lay fallow, but the wife was till'd.

ELIJAH FENTON

TO CHLOE

I could resign that eye of blue
  Howe'er its splendour used to thrill me;
And even that cheek of roseate hue, –
  To lose it, Chloe, scarce would kill me.

That snowy neck I ne'er should miss,
  However much I've raved about it;
And sweetly as that lip can kiss,
  I *think* I could exist without it.

In short, so well I've learned to fast,
  That, sooth my love, I know not whether
I might not bring myself at last,
  To – do without you altogether.

Villa Catulli

Villa Horatii

Villa Quintilii Vari

Templum Sibyllae

Pons Aquae cureus

Villa Maecenatis

Tibur

Villa Catlii

Fons Celius

Villa Salluftii

Via Sabina

Sepulcrum Plautiorum

Pons L...

Lapidicina Tiburtina, quae lapides suppeditavit ad urbis Romae fabricas.

Villa L. Centronii

JUVENAL

THE VANITY OF HUMAN
WISHES
The Tenth Satire of Juvenal Imitated

Let Observation with extensive View,
Survey Mankind from *China* to *Peru*;
Remark each anxious Toil, each eager Strife,
And watch the busy Scenes of crouded Life;
Then say how Hope and Fear, Desire and Hate,
O'erspread with Snares the clouded Maze of Fate,
Where wav'ring Man, betray'd by vent'rous Pride,
To trend the dreary Paths without a Guide;
As treach'rous Phantoms in the Mist delude,
Shuns fancied Ills, or chases airy Good.
How rarely Reason guides the stubbon Choice,
Rules the bold Hand, or prompts the suppliant Voice,
How Nations sink, by darling Schemes oppress'd,
When Vengeance listens to the Fool's Request.
Fate wings with ev'ry Wish th'afflictive Dart,
Each Gift of Nature, and each Grace of Art,
With fatal Heat impetuous Courage glows,
With fatal Sweetness Elocution flows,
Impeachment stops the Speaker's pow'rful Breath,
And restless Fire precipitates on Death.

But scarce observ'd the Knowing and the Bold,
Fall in the gen'ral Masscare of Gold;
Wide-wasting Pest! that rages unconfin'd,

And crouds with Crimes the Records of Mankind,
For Gold his Sword the Hireling Ruffian draws,
For Gold the hireling Judge distorts the Laws;
Wealth heap'd on Wealth, nor Truth nor Safety buys,
The Dangers gather as the Tresures rise.

    Let Hist'ry tell where rival Kings command,
And dubious Title shakes the madded Land,
When Statutes glean the Refuse of the Sword,
How much more safe the Vassal than the Lord,
Low sculks the Hind beneath the Rage of Pow'r,
And leaves the wealthy Traytor in the *Tow'r*,
Untouch'd his Cottage, and his Slumbers sound,
Tho' Confiscation's Vulturs hover round.

    The needy Traveller, serene and gay,
Walks the wild Heath, and sings his Toil away.
Does Envy seize thee? crush th'upbraiding Joy,
Encrease his Riches and his Peace destroy,
Now Fears in dire Vicissitude invade,
The rustling Brake alarms, and quiv'ring Shade,
Nor Light nor Darkness bring his Pain Relief,
One shews the Plunder, and one hides the Thief.

    Yet still one gen'ral Cry the Skies assails
And Gain and Granduer load the tainted Gales;
Few know the toiling Stateman's Fear or Care,
Th'insidious Rival and the gaping Heir.

    Once more, *Democritus*, arise on Earth,
With chearful Wisdom and instructive Mirth,

See motley Life in Modern Trappings dress'd,
And feed with varied Fool's th'eternal Jest:
Thou who couldst laugh where Want enchain'd
      Caprice,
Toil crush'd Conceit, and Man was of a Piece;
Where Wealth unlov'd without a Mourner dy'd;
And scarce a Sycophant was fed by Pride;
Where ne'er was known the Form of mock Debate,
Or seen a new-made Mayor's unwieldy State;
Where change of Fav'rites made no Change of Laws,
And Senates heard before they judg'd a Cause;
How wouldst thou shake at *Britain's* modish Tribe,
Dart the quick Taunt, and edge the piercing Gibe?
Attentive Truth and Nature to descry,
And pierce each Scene with Philosophic Eye.
To thee were solemn Toys or empty Shew,
The Robes of Pleasure and the Veil of Woe:
All aid the Farce, and all thy Mirth maintain,
Whose Joys are causeless, or whose Griefs are vain.

    Such was the Scorn that fill'd the Sage's Mind,
Renew'd at ev'ry Glance on Humankind;
How just that Scorn ere yet thy Voice declare,
Search every State, and canvass ev'ry Pray'r.

    Unnumber'd Suppliants croud Preferment's Gate,
Athirst for Wealth, and burning to be great;
Delusive Fortune hears th'incessant Call,
They mount, they shine, evaporate, and fall.

On ev'ry Stage the Foes of Peace attend,
Hate dogs their Flight, and Insult mocks their End.
Love ends with Hope, the sinking Statesman's Door
Pours in the Morning Worshiper no more;
For growing Names the weekly Scribbler lies,
To growing Wealth the Dedicator flies,
From every Room descends the painted Face,
That hung the bright *Palladium* of the Place,
And smoak'd in Kitchens, or in Auctions sold,
To better Features yields the Frame of Gold;
For now no more we trace in ev'ry Line
Heroic Worth, Benevolence Divine:
The Form distorted justifies the Fall,
And Detestation rids th'indignant Wall.

    But will not *Britain* hear the last Appeal,
Sign her Foes Doom, or guard her Fav'rites Zeal;
Through Freedom's Sons no more Remonstrance
      rings,
Degrading Nobles and controuling Kings;
Our supple Tribes repress their Patriot Throats,
And ask no Questions but the Price of Votes;
With Weekly Libels and Septennial Ale,
Their Wish is full to riot and to rail.

    In full-blown Dignity, see *Wolsey* stand,
Law in his Voice, and Fortune in his Hand:
To him the Church, the Realm, their Pow'rs consign,
Thro' him the Rays of regal Bounty shine,

Turn'd by his Nod the Stream of Honour flows,
His Smile alone Security bestows:
Still to new Heights his restless Wishes tow'r,
Claim leads to Claim, and Pow'r advances Pow'r;
Till Conquest unresisted ceas'd to please,
And Rights submitted, left him none to seize.
At length his Sov'reign frowns - the Train of State
Mark the keen Glance, and watch the Sign to hate.
Where-e'er he turns he meets a Stranger's Eye,
His Suppliants scorn him, and his Followers fly;
At once is lost the Pride of aweful State,
The golden Canopy, the glitt'ring Plate,
The regal Palace, the luxurious Board,
The liv'ried Army, and the menial Lord.
With Age, with Cares, with Maladies oppress'd,
He seeks the Refuge of Monastic Rest.
Grief aids Disease, remember'd Folly stings,
And his last Sighs reproach the Faith of Kings.
    Speak thou, whose Thoughts at humble Peace
        repine,
Shall *Wolsey*'s Wealth, with *Wolsey*'s End be thine?
Or liv'st thou now, with safer Pride content,
The wisest Justice on the Banks of *Trent*?
For why did *Wolsey* near the Steeps of Fate,
On weak Foundations raise th'enormous Weight?
Why but to sink beneath Misfortune's Blow,
With louder Ruin to the Gulphs below?

What gave great *Villiers* to th'Assassin's Knife,
And fixed Disease on *Harley*'s closing Life?
What murder'd *Wentworth*, and what exil'd *Hyde*,
By Kings protected and to Kings ally'd?
What but their Wish indulg'd in Courts to shine,
And Pow'r too great to keep or to resign?

When first the College Rolls receive his Name,
The young Enthusiast quits his Ease for Fame;
Through all his Veins the Fever of Renown
Burns from the strong Contagion of the Gown;
O'er *Bodley*'s Dome his future Labours spread,
And *Bacon*'s Mansion trembles o'er his Head;
Are these thy Views? proceed, illustrious Youth,
And Virtue guard to thee to the Throne of Truth,
Yet should thy Soul indulge the gen'rous Heat,
Till captive Science yields her last Retreat;
Should Reason guide thee with her brightest Ray,
And pour on misty Doubt resistless Day;
Should no false Kindness lure to loose Delight,
Nor Praise relax, nor Difficulty fright;
Should tempting Novelty thy Cell refrain,
And Sloth effuse her opiate Fumes in vain;
Should Beauty blunt on Fops her fatal Dart,
Nor claim the Truimph of a letter'd Heart;
Should no Disease thy torpid Veins invade,
Nor Melancholy's Phantoms haunt thy Shade;
Yet hope not Life from Grief or Danger free,

Nor think the Doom of Man revers'd for thee:
Deign on the passing World to turn thine Eyes,
And pause awhile from Letters to be wise;
There mark what Ills the Scholar's Life assail,
Toil, Envy, Want, the Patron, and the Jail.
See Nations slowly wise, and meanly just,
To buried Merit raise the tardy Bust.
If Dreams yet flatter, once again attend,
Hear *Lydiat*'s Life and *Galileo*'s End.

Nor deem, when Learning her last Prize bestows
The glitt'ring Eminence exempt from Foes;
See when the Vulgar 'scapes, despis'd or aw'd,
Rebellion's vengeful Talons seize on *Laud*.
From meaner Minds, tho' smaller Fines content
The plunder'd Palace or sequester'd Rent;
Mark'd out by dangerous Parts he meets the Shock,
And fatal Learning leads him to the Block:
Around his Tomb let Art and Genius weep,
But hear his Death, ye Blockheads, hear and sleep.

The festal Blazes, the triumphal Show,
The ravish'd Standard, and the captive Foe,
The Senate's Thanks, the Gazette's pompous Tale,
With Force resistless o'er the Brave prevail.
Such Bribes the rapid *Greek* o'er *Asia* whirl'd,
For such the steady *Romans* shook the World;
For such in distant Lands the *Britons* shine,
And stain with Blood the *Danube* or the *Rhine*;

This Pow'r has Praise, that Virtue scarce can warm,
Till Fame supplies the universal Charm.
Yet Reason frowns on War's unequal Game,
Where wasted Nations raise a single Name,
And mortgag'd States their Grandsires Wreaths
    regret
From Age to Age in everlasting Debt;
Wreaths which at last the dear-bought Right convey
To rust on Medals, or on Stones decay.
   On what Foundation stands the Warrior's Pride?
How just his Hopes let *Swedish Charles* decide;
A Frame of Adamant, a Soul of Fire,
No Dangers fright him, and no Labours tire;
O'er Love, o'er Fear, extends his wide Domain,
Unconquer'd Lord of Pleasure and of Pain;
No Joys to him pacific Scepter's yield,
War sounds the Trump, he rushes to the Field;
Behold surrounding Kings their Pow'rs combine,
And One capitulate, and One resign;
Peace courts his Hand, but spreads her Charms in vain;
'Think Nothing gain'd, he cries, till nought remain,
On *Moscow*'s Walls till *Gothic* Standards fly,
And all be Mine beneath the Polar Sky.'
The March begins in Military State,
And Nations on his Eye suspended wait;
Stern Famine guards the solitary Coast,
And Winter barricades the Realms of Frost;

He comes, nor Want nor Cold his Course delay;-
Hide, blushing Glory, hide *Pultowa*'s Day:
The vanquish'd Hero leaves his broken Bands,
And shews his Miseries in distant Lands;
Condemn'd a needy Supplicant to wait,
While Ladies interpose, and Slaves debate.
But did not Chance at length her Error mend?
Did no subverted Empire mark his End?
Did rival Monarchs give the fatal Wound?
Or hostile Millions press him to the Ground?
His Fall was destin'd to a barren Strand,
A petty Fortress, and a dubious Hand;
He left the Name, at which the World grew pale,
To point a Moral, or adorn a Tale.
   All Times their Scenes of pompous Woes afford,
From *Persia*'s Tyrant to *Bavaria*'s Lord.
In gay Hostility, and barb'rous Pride,
With half Mankind embattled at his Side,
Great *Xerxes* comes to seize the certain Prey,
And starves exhausted Regions in his Way;
Attendant Flatt'ry counts his Myriads o'er,
Till counted Myriads sooth his Pride no more;
Fresh Praise is try'd till Madness fires his Mind,
The Waves he lashes, and enchains the Wind;
New Pow'rs are claim'd, new Pow'rs are still bestow'd,
Till rude Resistance lops the spreading God;
The darling *Greeks* deride the Martial Shew,

And heap their Vallies with the gaudy Foe;
Th'insulted Sea with humbler Thoughts he gains,
A single Skiff to speed his Flight remains;
Th'incumber'd Oar scarce leaves the dreaded Coast
Through purple Billows and a floating Host.

    The bold *Bavarian*, in a luckless Hour,
Tries the dread Summits of *Cesarean* Pow'r,
With unexpected Legions bursts away,
And sees defenceless Realms receive his Sway;
Short Sway! fair *Austria* spreads her mournful Charms,
The Queen, the Beauty, sets the World in Arms;
From Hill to Hill the Beacons rousing Blaze
Spreads wide the Hope of Plunder and of Praise;
The fierce *Croatian*, and the wild *Hussar*,
With all the Sons of Ravage croud the War;
The baffled Prince in Honour's flatt'ring Bloom
Of hasty Greatness finds the fatal Doom,
His Foes Derision, and his Subjects Blame,
And steals to Death from Anguish and from Shame.

    Enlarge my life with Multitude of Days,
In Health, in Sickness, thus the Suppliant prays;
Hides from himself his State, and shuns to know,
That Life protracted is protracted Woe.
Time hovers o'er, impatient to destroy,
Ands shuts up all the Passages of Joy:
In vain their Gifts the bounteous Seasons pour,
The Fruit Autumnal, and the Vernal Flow'r,

With listless Eyes the Dotard views the Store,
He views, and wonders that they please no more;
Now pall the tastless Meats, and joyless Wines,
And Luxury with Sighs her Slave resigns.
Approach, ye Minstrels, try the soothing Strain,
Diffuse the tuneful Lenitives of Pain:
No Sound alas would touch th'impervious Ear,
Though dancing Mountains witness'd *Orpheus* near;
Nor Lute nor Lyre his feeble Pow'rs attend,
Nor sweeter Musick of a virtuous Friend,
But everlasting Dictates croud his Tongue,
Perversely grave, or positively wrong.
The still returning Tale, and ling'ring Jest,
Perplex the fawning Niece and pamper'd Guest,
While growing Hopes scare awe the gath'ring Sneer,
And scarce a Legacy can bribe to hear;
The watchful Guests still hint the last Offence,
The Daughter's Petulance, the Son's Expence,
Improve his heady Rage with treach'rous Skill,
And mould his Passions till they make his Will.

    Unnumber'd Maladies his Joints invade,
Lay Siege to Life and press the dire Blockade;
But unextinguish'd Av'rice still remains,
And dreaded Losses aggravate his Pains;
He turns, with anxious Heart and cripled Hands,
His Bonds of Debt, and Mortgages of Lands;
Or views his Coffers with suspicious Eyes,

Unlocks his Gold, and counts it till he dies.
    But grant, the Virtues of a temp'rate Prime
Bless with an Age exempt from Scorn or Crime;
An Age that melts with unperceiv'd Decay,
And glides in modest Innocence away;
Whose peaceful Day Benevolence endears,
Whose Night congratulating Conscience cheers;
The gen'ral Fav'rite as the gen'ral Friend:
Such Age there is, and who shall wish its End?
    Yet ev'n on this her Load Misfortune flings,
To press the weary Minutes flagging Wings:
New Sorrow rises as the Day returns,
A Sister sickens, or a Daughter mourns.
Now Kindred Merit fills the sable Bier,
Now lacerated Friendship claims a Tear.
Year chases Year, Decay pursues Decay,
Still drops some Joy from with'ring Life away;
New Forms arise, and diff'rent Views engage,
Superfluous lags the Vet'ran on the Stage,
Till pitying Nature signs the last Release,
And bids afflicted Worth retire to Peace.
    But few there are whom Hours like these await,
Who set unclouded in the Gulphs of Fate.
From *Lydia*'s Monarch should the Search descend,
By *Solon* caution'd to regard his End,
In Life's last Scene what Prodigies surprise,
Fears of the Brave, and Follies of the Wise?

From *Marlb'rough*'s Eyes the Streams of Dotage flow,
And *Swift* expires a Driv'ler and a Show.
  The teeming Mother, anxious for her Race,
Begs for each Birth the Fortune of a Face:
Yet *Vane* could tell what Ills form Beauty spring;
And *Sedley* curs'd the Form that pleas'd a King.
Ye Nymphs of rosy Lips and radiant Eyes,
Whom Pleasure keeps too busy to be wise,
Whom Joys with soft Varieties invite
By Day the Frolick, and the Dance by Night,
Who frown with Vanity, who smile with Art,
And ask the latest Fashion of the Heart,
What Care, what Rules your heedless Charms
        shall save,
Each Nymph your Rival, and each Youth your Slave?
Against your Fame with Fondness Hate combines,
The Rival batters, and the Lover mines.
With distant Voice neglected Virtue calls,
Less heard, and less the faint Remonstrance falls;
Tir'd with Contempt, she quits the slipp'ry Reign,
And Pride and Prudence take her Seat in vain.
In croud at once, where none the Pass defend,
The harmless Freedom, and the private Friend.
The Guardians yield, by Force superior ply'd;
To Int'rest, Prudence; and to Flatt'ry, Pride.
Here Beauty falls betray'd, despis'd, distress'd,
And hissing Infamy proclaims the rest.

Where then shall Hope and Fear their Objects find?
Must dull Suspence corrupt the stagnant Mind?
Must helpless Man, In Ignorance sedate,
Roll darkling down the Torrent of his Fate?
Must no Dislike alarm, no Wishes rise,
No Cries invoke the Mercies of the Skies?
Enquier, cease, Petitions yet remain,
Which Heav'n may hear, nor deem Religion vain.
Still raise for Good, the supplicating Voice,
But leave to Heav'n the Measure and the Choice.
Safe in his Pow'r, whose Eyes discern afar
The secret Ambush of a specious Pray'r.
Implore his Aid, in his Decisions rest,
Secure whate'er he gives, he gives the best.
Yet when the Sense of sacred Presence fires,
And strong Devotion to the Skies aspires,
Pour fourth thy Fervours for a healthful Mind,
Obeident Passions, and a Will resign'd;
For Love, which scarce collective Man can fill;
For Patience sov'reign o'er transmuted Ill;
For Faith, that panting for a happier Seat,
Counts Death kind Nature's Signal of Retreat:
These Goods for Man the Laws of Heav'n ordain,
These Goods he grants, who grants the Pow'r to gain;
With these celestial Wisdom calms the Mind,
And makes the Happiness she does not find.

EVEN BON

AUSONIUS

ON HIS COUSIN,
JULIA IDALIA

Idalia, poor child, is gone,
   Poor child, who might have been
A goddess fair to gaze upon
   As that Idalian Queen.

Sweet cousin (almost could I say
   Sister) to thy small shade
This only due that I can pay
   In song, and tears, is paid.

ANONYMOUS

ON HECTOR'S GRAVE

This is the grave of Hector: Troy lies in this
    small room —
The men, and the topless towers, that perished
    in his doom.

ANONYMOUS

THE FIELDS OF SORROW

They wander in deep woods, in mournful light,
Amid long reeds and drowsy-headed poppies,
And lakes where no wave laps, and voiceless streams,
Upon whose banks in the dim light grow old
Flowers that were once bewailed names of kings.

HELEN WADDELL

EVENING ON THE
MOSELLE

What colour are they now, thy quiet waters?
The evening star has brought the evening light,
And filled the river with the green hillside;
The hill-tops waver in the rippling water,
Trembles the absent vine and swells the grape
In thy clear crystal.

TO HIS WIFE

Love, let us live as we have lived, nor lose
    The little names that were the first night's grace,
And never come the day that sees us old,
    I still your lad, and you my little lass.
Let me be older than old Nestor's years,
    And you the Sibyl, if we heed it not.
What should we know, we two, of ripe old age?
    We'll have its richness, and the years forgot.

HELEN WADDELL

ROSES

'Twas Spring, and bitter-sweet the saffron morn
Blew hot and cold from Amalthea's horn.
A brisker gale usher'd Aurora's ray,
And bade her steeds outstrip the winged day.
Between the gardens' water'd beds I went,
Apollo's growing fury to prevent.
On the bent grass I saw congealed drops
And crystal pendants on the pot-herbs' tops.
Broad cabbages from leaf to leaf distill'd
The orient pearl, and all their bottles fill'd.
The hoary fruit-trees here and there a gem
Had candied o'er, to melt with the first beam.

The rose-trees in their Paestan scarlet laught,
And with red lips the morning's nectar quaft.
'Tis doubted whether Hesper borrowed
Or lent that paint, and dyed the roses red:
One dew, one colour, one celestial power
Of both, for they are Venus' star and flower.
Perchance one odour too, but *that*, being high,
Expires i' the air: *this* throws her incense nigh.
The Paphian mistress of the flower and star
Bade both her servants the same livery wear.
The moment came when on opposed banks
The flowery squadrons plac'd themselves in ranks.
One lay conceal'd in her leaves' close green hood,

Another peeping through the lattice stood.
This opes her first aspiring pyramid,
And ends it in a crimson pointed head.
That loos'd her garment (gather'd in her lap)
And in her native silks her self did wrap,
Uncovers now her laughing cup, and shows
The golden tuft which in her bottom grows.
She, that but now shone drest in all her hair,
Stands pale, forsook ev'n by those leaves she bare.

   So sudden change I wonder'd to behold,
And roses in their infancy grown old.
Whilst I speak this, those envied Beauties shed
Their glorious locks – earth cover'd with their dead.
So many kinds, so many births of flowers,
One day discloses, and one day devours.
Nature, why mad'st thou fading flowers so gay?
Why showd'st us gifts, to snatch them straight away?
A day's a rose's age. How near do meet
(Poor bloom!) thy cradle and thy winding-sheet!
Her whom the rising sun saw newly born,
He sees a wither'd corpse at his return.
Yet well with them, who, though they quickly die,
Survive themselves in their posterity.

   Gather your roses, Virgins, whilst they're new:
   For, being past, no Spring returns to you.

CLAUDIA

CLAUDIAN

THE OLD MAN OF VERONA

Happy the man, who his whole time doth bound
Within th' enclosure of his little ground.
Happy the man, whom the same humble place
(Th' hereditary cottage of his race)
From his first rising infancy has known,
And by degrees sees gently bending down,
With natural propension to that Earth
Which both preserv'd his life, and gave him birth.
Him no false distant lights, by fortune set,
Could ever into foolish wanderings get.
He never dangers either saw, or fear'd:
The dreadful storms at sea he never heard.
He never heard the shrill alarms of war,
Or the worse noises of the lawyer's bar.
No change of Consuls marks to him the year,
The change of seasons is his calendar.
The cold and heat winter and summer shows,
Autumn by fruits and spring by flowers he knows.
He measures time by land-marks, and has found
For the whole day the dial of his ground.
A neighbouring wood born with himself he sees,
And loves his old contemporary trees.
H'as only heard of near Verona's name,
And knows it like the Indies, but by fame.
Does with a like concernment notice take

Of the Red Sea, and of Benacus Lake.
Thus health and strength he to a third age enjoys,
And sees a long posterity of boys.
About the spacious world let others roam,
The voyage Life is longest made at home.

THE MAGNET

Who in the world with busy reason pries,
Searching the seed of things, and there descries
With what defect labours th' eclipsed moon,
What cause commands a paleness in the sun,
Whence ruddy comets with their fatal hair,
Whence winds do flow, and what the motions are
That shake the bowels of the trembling earth,
What strikes the lightning forth, whence clouds
    give birth
To horrid thunders, and doth also know
What light lends lustre to the painted bow –
If ought of truth his soul doth understand,
Let him resolve a question I'll demand.
    There is a stone which we the loadstone style,
Of colour ugly, dark, obscure and vile:
It never deck'd the sleeked locks of kings,
No ornament, no gorgeous tire it brings
To virgins' beauteous necks; it never shone
A splendent buckle in their maiden zone.
But only hear the wonders I will tell
Of this black pebble, and 'twill then excel
All bracelets, and whate'er the diving Moor
'Mongst the red weeds seeks for i' th' Eastern shore.
From iron first it lives; iron it eats.
But that sweet feast, it knows no other meats.

Thence she renews her strength; vigour is sent
Through all her nerves by that hard nourishment.
Without that food she dies: a famine numbs
Her meagre joints, a thirst her veins consumes.

    Mars that frights cities with his bloody spears,
And Venus, that releases human fears,
Do both together in one temple shine,
Both jointly honour'd in a common shrine;
But different statues, Mars a steel put on,
And Venus' figure was magnetic stone.
To them (as is the custom every year)
The priest doth celebrate a nuptial there.
The torch the quire doth lead, the threshold's green
With hallow'd myrtles, and the beds are seen
To smell with rosy flowers, the genial sheet
Spread over with a purple coverlet.

    But here (O strange!) the statues seem'd to move,
And Cytherea runs to catch her love:
And like their former joys in heaven possest,
With wanton heat clings to her Mars's breast:
There hangs a grateful burden: then she throws
Her arms about his helmet, to enclose
Her love in amorous gyves: lest he get out,
Her live embraces chain him round about.
He, stir'd with love breath'd gently through his veins,
Is drawn by unseen links and secret chains
To meet his spoused gem; the air doth wed

The steel unto the stone: thus strangely led,
The deities their stol'n delights replay'd,
And only Nature was the bridal maid.

What heat in these two metals did inspire
Such mutual league? what concord's powerful fire
Contracted their hard minds? the stone doth move
With amorous heat, the steel doth learn to love.
So Venus oft the god of war withstood,
And gives him milder looks, when hot with blood
He rages to the fight, fierce with desire,
And with drawn points whets up his active ire.
She dares go forth alone, and boldly meet
His foaming steeds, and with a winning greet
The tumour of his high-swollen breast assuage,
Tempering with gentle flames his violent rage.
Peace courts his soul, the fight he disavows,
And his red plumes he now to kisses bows.
    Ah, cruel boy! large thy dominions be;
The gods and all their thunders yield to thee;
Great Jove to leave his heaven thou canst constrain,
And midst the brinish waves to low again.
Now the cold rocks thou strik'st, the senseless stone
Thy weapon feels; a lustful heat doth run
Through veins of flint; the steel thy power can tame,
And rigid marble must admit thy flame.

THOMAS RANDOLPH   245

INDEX OF
TRANSLATORS

ACKNOWLEDGMENTS

Thanks are due to the following copyright holders for permission to reprint:

DAY-LEWIS, C.: Extract from *Virgil: Georgic 4*, translated by C. Day-Lewis, published by Jonathan Cape. Reprinted by permission of The Peters Fraser and Dunlop Group Ltd on behalf of The Estate of C. Day-Lewis. ELLIOT, ALISTAIR: 'Epigrams 1, 4: Caesar' by Martial, translated by Alistair Elliot, published by Carcanet Press Limited. HARRISON, TONY: 'Epigrams V, 9: A slight cold', by Martial, translated by Tony Harrison. © Tony Harrison. Reprinted by permission of Gordon Dickerson. HOUSMAN, A. E.: 'Horace: Odes IV, 7', translated by A. E. Housman, reprinted by permission of the Society of Authors as the Literary Representative of the Estate of A. E. Housman. LEE, GUY: 'Elegies II 29A, II 29B, and IV 7', from *Propertius: The Poems* translated by Guy Lee (1994). Reprinted by permission of Oxford University Press. MICHIE, JAMES: 'Carmen 15, 36, 42 and 56', from *The Poems of Catullus* translated by James Michie. © James Michie. Reprinted by permission of James Michie. PORTER, PETER: 'Epigram IX 54', from *After Martial* translated by Peter Porter (1972). Reprinted by permission of Oxford University Press.